:

Let No Chance Go Unseized:

The Life of St. Dominic Savio

Carolyn Cooney

ISBN: 9798719642093

for Our Lady and my brothers, especially Dominic Savio

"Let no chance of doing good to souls or offering some little sacrifice to God
be missed."

St. Dominic Savio

Prologue

A black-cassocked priest walked briskly through the dirty streets of Turin, Italy. A red sunset streaked the sky over the outline of dark, closely packed buildings. Vendors and store-owners hailed him warmly as they closed their shops for the day.

"Say a prayer for me tonight, Father!"

"Of course, of course! And you say one for me!"

A crowd of ragged boys tore across the road shouting and vanished into an alleyway. Boys...boys...how to help them, how to save their souls! There were so many of them – penniless, uneducated orphans who knew so little of the things that really mattered – shoved into homelessness and crime even as young as five or six years old, without having learned as much as how to make the Sign of the Cross...scores of them in jail, scores of them slaving in inhumane working conditions, scores of them in states of mortal sin. Yet all they needed and wanted was love, whether they knew it or not. How to help them, how to save their souls...

A frank, laughing face flitted into his mind. Clear and smiling grey-blue eyes; simple brown hair; that old determined mouth that knew what it wanted and wasn't afraid to speak up for it; the air of sincerity and modesty mixed with flaming passion and unquenchable grit — it all came back to him as if the lad were once again standing in front of him. Yes, here was a boy who had fulfilled his mission, who, unlike so many of his peers, had refused to yield to impurity. Here was a loyal friend and an ideal of youthful sainthood to offer to the searching souls of Turin — as he had been in life, so he would be in death. A champion of purity, a rock of friendship, a furnace of love, yet so normal in appearance; no wonder he had rescued so many straying souls. And if he could do it, so could the other boys. Sainthood was not reserved for a privileged few.

The priest had just reached the object of his journey when the door flung open and a frantic cleric rushed toward him.

"Don Bosco! Don Bosco!"

"What is it, my friend?"

"He's dying, Don Bosco! Hurry, hurry, if you want to see him before it's too late!"

"Who's dying?"

"Davico! It's his stomach — an awful seizure — hurry, Father, before he dies!"

"Ah, that Davico!" Don Bosco shook his head with an unconcerned smile on his lips. "He thinks he can go off like that without my permission, eh? Well, he's much mistaken. I haven't signed his passport."

The cleric, Father Alasonatti, simply looked at him in sheer helplessness.

A crowd of boys had filled the sickroom and raised wide eyes to Don

Bosco as he entered. One look at Davico was enough to assure the priest that the youngster was indeed on the brink of death. Kneeling at his bedside, he placed a tender hand on Davico's head and whispered a few words to him. Then he turned for a moment.

"All right, boys. Time to pray to Dominic Savio."

No sooner had they finished than Davico suddenly sat upright.

"I'm cured."

A startled shout went up from the boys. The doctor stared in disbelief, rubbed his eyes, cleaned his spectacles, pinched himself, rubbed his eyes again – all to no avail. Father Alasonatti gaped, muttering to himself in amazement. Could it be true?

"Three cheers for Savio!" someone cried.

"We knew he was a saint!"

A dozen hands reached to help the bewildered and ecstatic Davico from his bed, but Don Bosco stopped them.

"No!" he ordered, over the chaos of jubilance and astonishment. "If he wants to be cured, he'll have to get up himself."

The commotion trickled to a hush. It might be too much for him – there would be a relapse –.

"Nonsense," Don Bosco said firmly. "Come on now, Davico, get up! Dominic Savio doesn't do things by halves!"

One

A group of boys kicked up the dust on the road, laughing uproariously, their arms slung around each other's necks. They wore the faded cotton shirts and trousers of country village lads, and bundles of books strapped together by leather cords swung from their hands. There were six or seven of them, and they were all howling uncontrollably, so that the farmers they passed either looked up and grinned or else shook their pitchforks in surly annoyance.

"What an awful failure!" one of them was yelling. "Marco, Marco, I think you'd better join the circus!"

His remark was met with a storm of merriment.

"Yeah, Marco, one handspring and they'll take you on the spot!"

"They'll make you the ringleader, Marco!"

Marco was a good-natured fellow, and he laughed heartily with the rest of his friends. He knew his circus skills were far from professional, but who needed stellar abilities when one could get the same amount of attention by failing ludicrously? Marco was a practical boy.

His loudest tormentor, Luigi Abruzzo, was a black-haired, brawny farm lad with a reputation for spirit and mischief. Anywhere there was trouble, Luigi was bound to be in the middle of it, doubling over with laughter so contagious that few people could find the heart to punish him.

"Do it again, Marco!" Luigi cried.

"Yeah, do it again!" another boy urged, leaning on his friend's shoulder. This one had an open, easy-going expression and was poking a sprig of grass into his companion's face. "Need to practice for the circus, ya know!"

His friend, a dark-haired youngster with frank, smiling blue eyes, shoved away the tickling grass and elbowed him in the ribs. "Whad'ya mean, Angelo, he's good enough already! I'll bet he could turn a handspring clear over Signor Bottini's pig fence!"

The group fairly suffocated with laughter. Everyone knew how Signor Bottini had built such a tall fence for his unruly pigs that it stood up to the roof of his house.

"Aw, sure, I could spring that old fence with ease!" the unquenchable Marco boasted. "Just watch me now!"

"Mar-co! Mar-co!" they chanted, led on by the dark-haired boy. "Come on, old fellow! Mar-co! Mar-co!"

Marco dashed forward, placed his hands firmly on the ground, and launched his body over them zealously. For a whole moment his legs sailed promisingly through the air – then he landed with a dull *thud!* flat on his back.

The boys erupted into a wild cheer and rushed to pick him up and resume their comradely tormenting.

"Circus material right there, Marco!" Luigi shouted.

"Thank you, thank you!" Marco picked up his dusty cap from the ground and clapped it on his head so he could sweep it off again in a series of bows. "Ow, my back — thank you, thank you!"

It was that glorious afternoon hour of coming home from school, and they were in the highest moods. A cloudless blue sky soared overhead, and timid flowers were peeking from the soft earth, sending a spring itch through their bones. They chased each other, shoved each other, teased each other — perhaps it was this restless atmosphere or else the fact that he had just visited his questionable relatives in Turin, combined with his driving love for attention, that caused Marco Carabella to start telling a story undeniably off-color.

Angelo's dark-haired friend had been bent over laughing at one of Luigi's hare-brained jokes, but as he heard Marco's words, the blood rushed furiously into his face.

"Whoa, there, Marco! You know that's not right! C'mon, don't talk like that." His eyes were flashing dangerously, for even at ten years old, Dominic Savio would stand for nothing in the way of impurity.

He had stopped short in his tracks and stood tense like a lion daring its foe to fight. Marco paused. The jubilant boisterousness of the boys seemed to hold in its breath.

"Well..." Marco shifted his feet uncomfortably. He hadn't expected things to go this way. His mind raced to find a way out of the situation without apologizing, but knowing Dominic...

Just then Luigi broke in. "Let him be, Dom, I wanna hear the rest of the story."

"Oh no you don't!" Dominic declared brazenly. His fists were clenched until the knuckles were white.

"Yes, I do! And I *will* hear it, or else —." He stepped up to the smaller but wrathful boy with every muscle threateningly taut.

"You don't want to hear it, Luigi, and no one should stand around and listen to that kind of stuff. It's trash!"

A hard blow whistled through the air, and Dominic stumbled back bleeding. Only for a moment. The hot blood surging through his veins, he whirled forward and slammed his fist solidly into Luigi's jaw. The boys yelled in surprise and circled around the two opponents, waiting to see what would happen next. Luigi recovered and drew back his fist angrily. Dominic faced him belligerently – then, all of a sudden, he lowered his fists and turned away.

His young frame was still trembling with fury, but without saying a word he walked away in the direction they had come.

The group stood silent for a moment. Luigi cast sullen glances at his companions but found no sympathy written in their faces.

"Coward!" he muttered. "Running away from a fight."

"Leave him alone, won't you?" Angelo snapped. "He's much braver than you, and we all know it."

Luigi seemed ready to strike again, but the surly countenances around him counseled him otherwise. "Well, go on, Marco," he changed the subject gruffly. "He's gone, so finish telling your story."

Marco frowned and kicked a loose pebble. "I don't want to anymore."

———————

The village church was empty. Dominic stood in the doorway panting, for he had run the last part of the way. Reverently, he took off his cap and blessed himself. Then he walked slowly to the front of the church, his head hanging in shame. At the altar of Our Lady, he threw himself down on his knees and laid his head at the feet of her statue. The tears began to stream down unchecked.

"Oh, Mamma!" he sobbed heartbrokenly. "I'm so sorry! I wanted to honor you and defend you by stopping Marco from continuing that awful story, and instead I hurt you! And I hurt my Jesus, too...oh, help me, my Mamma! Help me to be good! How can I be truly good if I lose my temper all the time like this? And I fought with Raimonda — oh, help me out! I wish I didn't punch him, Mother, I wish with all my heart I didn't! If only I could control my temper, maybe I'd be able to do some good for your sake instead of just causing more trouble." He wiped his eyes inconsolably as another sob racked his boyish body. "Won't you help me, Mamma?"

What mother could resist such a plea? Surely not the Mother of God. Her gentle smile from her throne in heaven made its way down into the valley of tears and resided to warm her child's weeping heart. Of course she would help him. She had always been helping him, long before he had realized it. She had helped him turn away from the fight, and she would always be there, teaching him, guiding him, bringing him ever closer to Jesus — yes, she would make him good, wondrously good. He need not fear. Why fear when all is in the hands of your Mother? Be at ease, dearest child; do not be troubled... Would she keep him always free from mortal sin?... Yes, little one, if you will continue to fight it, free, always... I will fight it to the death, Mamma!

When Father Giovanni Zucca entered the church, he found the blood and tears still wet upon Dominic's face, but a peaceful smile shone upon his lips.

"Yes, Mamma," he was whispering. "For you, for Jesus! — death before sin!"

The priest hesitated. Perhaps he would have left quietly if not for the sight of the blood. That drove him to speak.

"Dominic!" he called in a low voice.

The boy drew himself slowly out of prayer as if it cost much effort and left the altar to greet the priest.

"Good afternoon, Father!"

"Who hurt you, Dominic?"

He reddened. "Don't mind me, Father. It was my fault. I wasn't kind enough."

So that was it, the pastor thought grimly. Evangelizing again, to his bodily peril. Well, it wasn't exactly in the order of things to stop it, but if he ever got hands on the real culprit...

"Very well, then," he said reluctantly. "That's all. God bless you, son."

"You too, Father!"

Dominic smiled his cheery old smile and started off toward home, his heart light once again.

Father Zucca watched him disappear down the road with a thoughtful expression. That young Savio was so different from the rest of the boys, he mused — so pure-minded, so devout, so remarkably honest, and so forcefully driven. Yet in some ways he was just like them, too. Friendly, cheerful, always ready to join in the games or have a good laugh — it was no wonder he was one of the most popular youngsters in Father Zucca's parish school. One could almost think at times that he was just like anyone else, and then something like this happened... The priest furrowed his brows and recalled an event of some years ago.

It had been a piercingly cold day. He was tramping through the knee-high snow with his hands shoved deep into his pockets. Once again, the blistering wind seemed to sting his ears. Shivering, he had hunched into his scarf and quickened his pace.

The morning was very early, and he had wondered how many people would be there to attend Mass. In weather like this, probably very few. He hadn't been a priest at the church in Murialdo very long then, and he was still getting to know some of the village people. They were good, hard-working people for the most part, but on a day like this... A harsh wind whipped through the marrows of his bones, and he wondered dimly if he would get frostbite.

The village church rose in the distance, with a dark blue sky stretching overhead. He hurried over the last steps and suddenly stopped in amazement.

"Why, Dominic! That's not you, is it?"

A five-year-old boy was kneeling in the snow in front of the church doors. When he heard the priest's voice, he looked up and gave him a tired yet bright-faced smile. As Father Zucca unlocked the doors, he glanced keenly at the boy rising painfully to his feet.

"Goodness, son!" he cried. "You're stiff with cold!"

Quickly, he wrapped an arm around the boy and half-carried him into the sacristy.

"I'm all right, Father," Dominic assured him, a bit embarrassed. "Compared to what He did for me..."

No, Father Zucca had not been at Murialdo long then, but at that point he had been there long enough to discover that little Dominic Savio was quite out of the ordinary. It didn't take an hour to find that much out. But it was that morning that he had realized the extent of the boy's flaming devotion. Snow knee high, the biting cold, the early hour...yet little Savio had been right. It was the Lord.

———————

Brigida Savio threw up her hands in horror when her son entered the house.

"Just look at your face, young man!" she exclaimed. "What on earth have you been up to?"

"I fought with Luigi," Dominic confessed remorsefully. "I'm sorry, Mamma. I won't do it again."

"I'm sure you won't!" she flung back grimly. "I wouldn't either, if I were you. He's a sight bigger than you."

She was drawing a fresh loaf of bread out of the oven, and Dominic seized his opportunity.

"Maybe you can help me there, Mamma," he suggested sweetly.

"Help you do what?"

"Why, help me grow!" He eyed the bread innocently.

"You young rascal!" she exclaimed, but laughing, gave him a slice of the bread and a slap with the end of her towel.

"How was school today?" she asked, as Dominic scooped up his baby brother Giovanni and sat him on his lap.

"Good," he mumbled, wolfing down the bread.

"Anything else you care to tell me?" she questioned drily.

Dominic grinned.

Brigida dusted off her floury hands on her apron and stood eyeing him for a moment.

"School's almost over, eh?" she commented. Swiftly, Dominic glanced up with anxious eyes, and his mother sighed. "I know you want to continue studying but we can't, child — we're too poor. If we had more money..."

"But, Mamma, I have to go to school!" The easy crinkles of laughter had vanished from his face, leaving a firm expression of determination.

Goodness, Brigida thought, why did the boy have to be so headstrong? Whenever he set his mind on something, it was almost impossible to distract him from it. Yet the memory of a frighteningly frail newborn child flitted through her head, and she admitted to herself that if it hadn't been for that persistent will power, and God's grace, of course, he might not have survived. Well, there was certainly something strong and single-minded in him, whether she liked it or not.

"Look, Dominic, you won't even be able to go back to Father Zucca's school. You'll be too old."

"There's Castelnuovo," he reminded her quietly.

"That's three miles away!" She flung her hands up in despair. "And down that horrible bandit-infested road, too!"

"I don't mind, Mamma. I just have to go to school."

She tried a new tactic. "I know you want to, but we need your help. You know how poor we are. Now that you're getting older, it's time we send you to learn a trade so you can help support the family. Oh, Dominic," she sighed earnestly, "we'd send you to school in a heartbeat if we could!"

Dominic stared morosely at the earthen floor and then at Giovanni's patched and faded clothes. They certainly were poor. It was hard to even get food on the table. As the oldest of his four siblings, he felt he had a responsibility to bring in some much-needed money, but then – he *had* to keep up his studies. A vague doubt clouded his mind, but then he heard the Heavenly Lady's voice speaking again in his heart: why fear when all is in the hands of your Mother? She would take care of his family better than he could. For his part –.

"Please let me go to school at Castelnuovo, Mom!" he begged in a low voice. "I have to study, if I'm going to become a priest."

Brigida Savio sighed again. She knew he wanted to be a priest. A noble desire, to be sure, but how could one be certain it wasn't just a childhood whim that would come to nothing? And yet...she gazed at his sincere face, and her heart softened. Perhaps – just perhaps – he really would become a priest, and what a great honor that would be! Her dear little Domenico a priest!

"Well, darling," she relented, "I'll ask your father to consider it. We'll see what he says. Now off with you, and give me space to think."

Dominic beamed and threw his arms around her neck in such a fashion that she had no choice but to return his winsome smile.

"Thank you, Mom!"

"You imp, you!" She ruffled his hair with rough tenderness. "Now out, I say!"

You are good, my Mamma! Jesus never refuses you, does He? Now only persuade Dad...

———————

"Sorry I punched you yesterday, Luigi. Shake on it?"

Luigi grabbed Dominic's hand readily. It was impossible to stay mad at him.

But Dominic didn't always get off as easily as that. Not long later, a group of village boys were rambling together through the fields. It was a warm spring day, and their stomachs were growling, but they didn't want to go home and get put to some odd jobs by their mothers.

"Tell you what," suggested Bruno Vastelli, a big fellow generally accepted as the village rascal. "Old Greco's orchards are just past that hill, and his apricots are starting to ripen. Some are still a bit green, but I daresay there are enough good ones to fill our bellies. Whad'ya say?"

"Sure, suits me!"

"I'd eat grass at this point."

"What if we get caught?"

"We run."

"Let's go, then. I'm starving!"

They started off enthusiastically, but one of them hung back. Bruno turned impatiently.

"C'mon, Savio, stop lagging!"

The younger boy braced himself. "I don't want to go, Bruno."

"Well, too bad. You're coming with us."

"I'd rather go home."

"Stop being a ninny, Savio!" someone yelled.

"Don't let him go home, Vastelli, or he'll tell on us!" another joined.

"What is it, too good for our company?" Bruno jeered.

"I can't steal," was Dominic's only answer.

If he was afraid, he did not show it. Biting his lips, he merely turned toward home.

In a flash, Bruno seized his collar and flung him to the ground.

"Don't let him escape, fellas!" he shouted. "We don't want any tattle tales!"

Dominic shielded his face as the boys leapt on him and covered him with stinging kicks and blows. He wasn't unused to this, but dearest Mamma — just don't let him hit back this time! Before long he was aching and bleeding all over, but he kept his fists tightly clenched together. He wouldn't hit back, he couldn't hurt them — his body rolled back and forth as he tried to get up but was only knocked back down.

Finally Bruno signaled them to stop. Breathing heavily, Dominic lay sprawled in the grass, his hands still balled in relentless determination. He squinted open a blackened eye and noticed a group of his friends standing by in a nervous huddle, too afraid to interfere. His eyes met Angelo's for a painful moment, and suddenly Angelo disappeared quietly beyond the hill.

"All right, Savio, now come with us," Bruno ordered, expecting to be obeyed.

Dominic glared at him. "You can kick me all you like, but I won't go. And I'm not going to tell on you either, but I tell you I won't steal!"

"You come with us!" Bruno snapped furiously.

"Aw, just leave him," one of the boys complained. "He's not gonna change his mind, and I'm hungry for those apricots."

They argued with each other for a few minutes, but before they came to a decision, a wrathful yell met their ears. Signor Greco, the orchard owner, was storming up the hill shaking a pitchfork in his horny hand.

"Get away from here, all of you!" he thundered, rattling the menacing weapon. "Out! Go! Don't you come near my property, or I'll —!"

They didn't wait to hear it. Characteristic of people with guilty consciences, they were too frightened to wait for even an accusation and took to their heels.

Signor Greco bawled a string of threats after them, then knelt next to the bruised and bleeding boy.

"You all right, sonny?" he demanded with gruff gentleness.

"Sure am, Signor. Don't bother about me!"

The hill was cleared of boys, but from behind a thick tree a familiar figure cautiously emerged.

"It's not too bad, is it, Dom?" Angelo asked hopefully, coming forward.

"Why, hello, Angelo! Don't worry, I've gotten worse!" Dominic assured him cheerfully.

He raised himself up on one elbow and winced. Sharp pain shot through his side. "That's where Our Lord had it," he muttered to himself between his teeth. "Give me a hand, won't you, Angelo?"

As Angelo helped him to his feet, the farmer rubbed his forehead thoughtfully.

"You'll be okay getting home?" he asked in concern.

"I will, don't worry!"

"Wait one minute!" Signor Greco suddenly commanded. He hurried off and a few minutes later returned with two orange, juicy apricots in his hands.

"Take these for the way home."

Dominic took one look at them and laughed until he could hardly breathe.

"God rewards well, doesn't He?" he grinned, biting into his fruit as they walked home. "A clear conscience and I got the apricot anyway!"

Angelo snorted. "You got a nice bucketload of bruises, too." He steadied his friend with a sturdy arm, as Dominic stumbled a little.

"Well, hey, Angelo!" Dominic returned merrily. "*You* did pretty well!"

"Yeah," Angelo agreed. He wiped a grim mouth on his sleeve. "But next time, Dom, I'm gonna knock them out or take the beating with you."

Carlo Savio laid down his hammer and mopped the sweat from his forehead. Summer was coming fast. And with the beginning of summer... He knit his brows in a muddle of indecision.

He had thought it over a hundred times, and had talked with Brigida and Dominic again and again, but he couldn't make up his mind. Sighing, he took up the hammer and pounded at the bar of red glowing metal. He loved his son dearly and hated to refuse him anything, but the family was so poor... Down went the hammer, and a flurry of sparks flew into the air.

The boy was bright, one had to admit, and it would be a shame to end his education so early. But then, other families like the Savios took their sons out of school at this age to earn money. That was the reality when you hardly had enough money to put food on the table. Carlo swung his hammer so hard that the metal broke. Frustrated, he picked up the pieces with his tongs and laid them on a tray, then held a new piece over the scorching fire. If only he could send his boy to school! Why was it that some people could send their stupid, rich children to school while smart kids like Dominic were destined to slave away in lives of poverty and ignorance? It simply wasn't fair.

Carlo wiped his forehead again with a sinking feeling of helplessness. Well, he couldn't change that. He had to think logically. Maybe Dominic could learn a trade as a blacksmith like himself, or a shoemaker, or −. The boy's pleading face rose before his mind.

"But, Dad, I need to study so I can become a priest," the earnest voice begged for the thousandth time.

A priest! Logic went out the window. His son couldn't become a priest roasting up in a smithy like this all day! But supposing he changed his mind? Every child held dreams for the future that changed as easily as the wind. A farmer one day, a soldier the next, then the governor – why not a priest? But Dominic wasn't like that, Carlo had to admit to himself. Dominic had always known exactly what he wanted. And he had nearly always been successful in getting it, too. Heaven help Carlo's savings!

Supposing he did send him to school, then – and mind you, he was just supposing. Merely idly speculating... That school in Castelnuovo was the closest one besides Father Zucca's school, which Dominic was now finishing. He'd have to walk three miles to get there, and it wouldn't be walking down a lane in the park, either. Carlo had heard enough stories of thieveries along that road to not want to take it himself. Of course, Dominic didn't seem concerned about it in the least, but what would a ten-year-old boy know about danger, anyway? Why, just the other day he had come home clothed in bruises from head to toe! If that was his idea of prudence and caution, saints preserve him. No, it just wasn't a good idea. He'd have to learn a trade.

Somewhat frustrated by his decision, Carlo tossed the piece of metal onto the anvil and wiped his grimy hands with a rag. He closed the shop for the day with a surly frown. At least he'd made up his mind. That was a relief.

On his way home, he passed the church. He signed himself before the doors, and as he did so, an image of the Virgin Mary appeared in his head. Suddenly he felt uncertain about himself.

When he reached home, he found his son kneeling in a corner of the house. His eyes were closed, and his face tranquil, so tranquil that Carlo hesitated to disturb him.

"I trust you, my Mamma," he was repeating softly. "Yes, I trust."

Abruptly, Carlo turned on his heel and left the small room. A priest...a priest...just what if it were true? And even if he didn't become a priest, what if it were simply God's Will that Dominic should study? "Dominic" – "of the Lord" – in a sense his son was not his own. His poor mind was in chaos all over again. Just what if...perhaps God would take care of His own...

Two months later, on the Feast of Saint Aloysius Gonzaga, June 21, 1852, Dominic attended his first day of classes at the school in Castelnuovo.

When the neighbors got wind that young Savio was going to school in Castelnuovo, they were thoroughly incensed.

"Just what is that family thinking?" they snapped to each other. "Sending their child straight into the arms of a robbers' den, that's what that is!"

When day after day Dominic was seen traipsing fearlessly toward Castelnuovo regardless of the scorching heat, the matronly gossip flared up even higher.

"He's going to kill himself, mark my words," Signora Carabella prophesied darkly.

"Or the thieves will do it for him," Signora Negri forebode.

"Three whole miles, mind you, and he makes the trip four times in a single day!" Signora Abruzzo jabbed four fingers into the air. "He'll faint from the heat someday, and no one will ever know it!"

"That's what I say, too." Signora Greco shook her head. "That Dominic is certainly no Hercules, and it would be asking a lot of a much stronger child!"

They were congregated on a few stacks of hay in the Carabellas' barn, as the younger people of the village swung themselves around in a lively barn dance. A violin trio fiddled away in a warmly lit corner. Outside, the warm wind blew through the open doors.

"I tell you what," Signora Vastelli declared emphatically, "one of us ought to put a stop to this nonsense before the boy kills himself. It's our duty as Christian neighbors."

"Well, what are we going to do, eh? Believe me, I've talked to that Brigida more than once, and she won't listen to a word I say. From what I've gathered, it was the boy's decision, and they're letting him have his way, the fools." Signora Negri pursed her lips in indignance that her invaluable advice had been ignored.

"I see," Signora Abruzzo nodded. "Coming from the boy, eh?"

"It's a wonder he hasn't given up already," murmured Signora Greco.

"He can be stubborn when he wants to, though why he'd want to in this case is beyond *me*." Signora Carabella looked over to where Dominic was standing, apparently protesting with some other boys. "If I'm not mistaken," she added, squinting, "it seems to me the walk is already showing on his health. Not that he was ever a Hercules, as our dear Marguerita said, but just look at him now! The wind could blow him away in one good puff! In fact, I'd say — what is it, Maria?"

Signora Abruzzo was clearing her throat ostentatiously. On receiving the desired attention, she spoke with the deliberate air of a judge. "I say, my good ladies, that we put our foot down. Of course, it's no use going to Brigida, as *she's* clearly out of her mind, so we'll go about it differently. We'll persuade her through the boy."

"What? But he's the one who wants it!"

"Exactly. So once he sees how foolish this all is, he'll tell his mother and she'll put an end to it for once and for all. Then he can learn something useful, instead of simply risking his skins for some worthless Latin."

"Persuade *him*." Signora Vastelli snorted. "It'd be easier to persuade my mule to pull a cart straight through the ocean to America than to persuade *him*."

Signora Abruzzo chose to ignore the remark. "Lucia," she said, addressing Signora Negri, "you live on his way to school, eh? Why don't you get your husband to give the boy a few drops of common sense? Just make conversation as he passes by, you know?"

Signora Negri nodded with a slow smile. "I rather like the idea. I'll tell him that."

A few raised voices interrupted their plotting. Around Dominic stood a handful of boys arguing with him and mocking him.

"C'mon, little priest!" one of them derided. "Dance for us!"

"Yea, dance! Dance!" the others chanted.

They were standing right next to a line of dancers and were about to shove him into it. His face upset but resolute, Dominic simply left them.

Watching him, Signora Greco remembered her husband's description of the bruises some of those boys had given him. She shook her head. "Signor Negri can talk to him until he's blue in the face," she said in a low voice. "I don't think he'll change Dominic's mind one bit."

Signor Negri stumped over his fields toward the fence that separated his farm from the road to Castelnuovo, feeling a bit disgruntled. Those old hens at it again. So the Savios wanted to send their boy to school. That was their business, not the hens', and certainly not his. Those gossiping village ladies would do their neighbors a sight more good by keeping their mouths shut. Well, anyway, he had promised, and here he was. Lands alive, but it was hot! He mopped his brow and panted as he reached the fence.

No one was in sight yet. He'd have to pretend to be doing something so it didn't look obvious that he meant to talk to Dominic about this silly business. He glanced around for work and found some dead vines clinging to his fence which he promptly began to tear off.

Soon the small, familiar figure appeared in the distance where the road met the sky, swinging his books contentedly. Signor Negri noticed that he was running out of vines to pull and hastily stopped so he would have enough left for when Dominic was there. Then, for nothing better to do, he patted the fence in various places, hoped it appeared that he was in fact doing something or other, and felt utterly ridiculous.

"Hello there, Dominic!" he called out, as the boy neared him.

"Hello, Signor Negri!" Dominic greeted him pleasantly.

He did look a little thinner than before, Signor Negri noticed.

"On your way to school?"

"Yes, sir."

"Aren't you afraid to take this road all alone every day? It's quite dangerous, you know."

"Oh, no, I'm not afraid at all!"

"No?" Signor Negri was quite surprised.

"Well, you see, I don't go alone. My guardian angel comes with me, and we talk things over."

"Ah! I see!" The old man felt baffled. "But you still must get pretty tired, especially on days like this, no?"

"I guess I would if I were doing it for myself. But nothing feels tiring or painful when you work for a Master Who pays well, you know."

"Who's that?"

"It's Our Lord, Who rewards even a cup of cold water given for love of Him."

Signor Negri felt his eyes going round. "Well, son, I won't keep you. Have a good day!"

"You too, sir!" Dominic doffed his cap with a friendly smile and walked on.

"Whew!" whistled the farmer, as Dominic's slight outline disappeared beyond the hills. "Wait 'til the hens hear that one!"

The hens were wonderfully flabbergasted.

"A boy who has thoughts like that at ten years old," Signor Negri concluded sagely, quietly enjoying their expressions of astonishment, "is sure destined for a great career."

Dominic's career was sainthood.

The story got around to Carlo Savio a few days later from a customer who dropped into the smithy. Of course, the customer made sure to leave out certain details such as the intent of the conversation, but the story lingered in the blacksmith's mind as he went about his work that morning.

So little Dominic talked things over with his guardian angel. Carlo had always wondered just what went through that head. Nor was he much surprised now that he knew.

A different story, however, kept running through his mind, triggered by his customer's account.

It had happened a while back, when he had taken Dominic to a festival in honor of one of the saints. The festival had been in a different town and had been full of movement, crowds, and energy, so that by the time they were walking home, Dominic was exhausted. After a whole day of running about and playing games in the whole-hearted way he always did, he could scarcely drag himself home.

Time and again Carlo paused to wait for him, growing increasingly uncomfortable. He didn't like to be out late like this – Brigida would be worried –.

Once again, he turned to wait for Dominic, who had fallen a few steps behind. He started at what he saw.

A handsome young man was standing by Dominic's side. As Carlo watched, confused, the youth gently took the boy into his arms and continued the journey toward home. Carlo's mind spun in bewilderment. He had never seen this man before, and yet the stranger gazed at his son with such tender familiarity that he clearly knew Dominic well. Dominic, meanwhile, had already fallen fast asleep, his head resting peacefully over the youth's heart.

The breeze was soft and warm, and as they neared home, Dominic stirred and flicked open his eyelids heavily. The young man smiled at him and set him down in front of the door while Carlo unlocked the bolt. When the blacksmith turned to thank the stranger, he was gone.

Mulling over this mysterious event, Carlo paused at his work to gaze through the window at the distant Alps, sloping in all their splendor. He had been nervous on his son's account, to have him walking down that dangerous road so often and all alone. But now he wasn't so nervous anymore. He picked up his hammer and swung it with a lightened heart. Dominic was right, he thought. He didn't go alone.

———

Dominic trudged through the cold, wet snow on his way to school. Something between rain and snow was whipping into his face, accompanied by a driving, stinging wind. He clung to his books with a red, chapped hand and kept the other one buried deep in his pocket.

"It's cold today," he remarked to his guardian angel. "You're lucky you can't feel it." He nestled his face further into his scarf. "Mom was talking to me about holy purity last night," he went on confidingly, "and I have some questions about it. First of all, why do some people not seem to want it at all? Don't they realize how important and beautiful it is?"

They don't see its importance and beauty at all, little one. They've become too distracted by worldly things, which they think are more important and beautiful than purity. You must pray for their souls.

Dominic's face grew troubled and serious. "If only people understood! We have to be pure to become saints, but there are so many people who lead impure lives. Don't they understand that God made them so they could become saints, and for no other reason?"

Some of them never learn that, Dominic, others forget it, and worst of all, many ignore it.

Would he ever forget or ignore it? Dominic's brows were knitted anxiously.

Not if you stay close to Our Lady.

He relaxed a little. "Yes, she will keep me good." Then he grew worried again. "She won't ever let me commit a mortal sin, will she? I'd rather die than hurt her in such a way."

You must pray and make sacrifices for holy purity. Offer these to her Immaculate Heart, and she will help you keep yourself always pure.

"You'll kill me if you see me about to commit a mortal sin, won't you?"

Guardian angels aren't exactly intended for killing their charges.

"Oh, you know what I mean!"

Dominic laughed as he started up a steep hill. But the thought of making sacrifices for holy purity was still fresh on his mind. He already prayed for this intention often, but what sacrifices could he offer?

The harsh wind swept down the hill and seemed to slice through his body. Each step took such effort, and his hands and feet felt on fire. His head bent down against the wind, he glanced at the hand carrying his books and found it covered in chilblains. But wait a minute —!

The chapel was almost empty when Dominic slipped into it a few minutes before class. Quietly, he made his way to the statue of Our Lady and presented to her two red, puffed-up hands.

"For you, my Mamma!" he whispered glowingly. "Keep me pure!"

Two

Dominic was sick. Months of walking twelve miles each day, completely exposed to the elements, had worn down the last threads of his already poor health. Feebly, he begged his mother to let him go to school, but to no avail.

"I've let you go when you were sick before," she answered firmly, "and just look where that got you. No, sir, you're staying right here."

Thus ended Dominic's days at Castelnuovo. That month, February of 1853, the Savios moved to the nearby town of Mondonio, so Carlo could take over the smithy of his recently deceased uncle. Once he had recovered, Dominic resumed his classes at the school there in Mondonio.

On his first day at the new school, he ran into a pleasant surprise.

"Hey, Angelo! Angelo! Is that you? What are you doing here?"

Delighted, Dominic leapt on his old friend in a bear hug.

"Why, Dom!" Angelo almost squeezed the life out of him. "What are *you* doing here?"

"We moved, so I'm going to school here. Now what are *you* doing here?"

"This school has higher grades than most of 'em, so I come every day from Murialdo. Father Cugliero is pretty tough, but we all like him. Well, most of us, anyway. Those fellows over there," he nudged a thumb toward a group of boys lounging idly against the wall, "they're up to no good. They always prank poor Father. That one with the red shirt, Antonio Di Marzio, is on the verge of being expelled. You'd do well to stay away from them. And now!" Angelo mounted a tall stump and waved his arms in the air. "Hey, hey!" he bawled out. "I have an announcement! We have a new classmate!" Already a throng of boys were gathering around them. "Dominic Savio, fellows!"

"He your cousin or somethin', Angelo?" someone asked.

Angelo and Dominic had the same last name, though they weren't related.

Dominic didn't crack a smile. "Long lost brothers," he answered.

Needless to say, the Mondonio boys took to Dominic right away. It wasn't long before the whole school knew and loved him. Bright and hardworking, thoughtful and kind, a zealous playmate and a cheerful friend, he easily won over their hearts. Not least of all that attracted them to him was his holiness. Nothing attracts the human heart as does genuine, committed holiness. Nor does anything attract so much attention.

Dominic got this attention, all right. The boys flocked to him as their friend. He also got it from the group of fellows Angelo had warned him against.

One morning he arrived at school early since it was his turn to prepare the fire stove before class. Before the doors of the building, he found his schoolmates engaged in an intense snowball fight. Slushy balls of ice whizzed every which way.

"Come join us, Savio!" someone urged, flinging a snowball at him.

Swiftly, Dominic scooped up a snowball and took his revenge, then retreated reluctantly. "Gotta fix up the stove!" he called back.

The band of troublemakers were in the thick of the battle, but at Dominic's words, one of them looked up abruptly and whispered something into the ear of the next. One by one, the whole group disappeared from the fight, so cunningly that no one noticed their departure.

In the classroom it was freezing cold. Dominic left his books on his desk and knelt before the stove to rake out the ashes from yesterday's fire. Funny how fire could turn hard chunks of wood into this soft, powdery stuff. Outside, the yells of his classmates drifted through the window. Maybe if he hurried, he could join them. The stove clean, he went to the woodpile and set to work building a sturdy pyramid of firewood over the kindling. Now, let's see, did he remember his lessons? Julius Caesar was assassinated on the Ides of March, 44 BC —.

A scuffle at the door caught his attention. Antonio Di Marzio swaggered into the room and planted himself before Dominic, his arms crossed commandingly over his chest.

"Now, my friend, we're gonna have a little fun. If you'll kindly get out of the way and keep your mouth shut, you won't get beat up."

Roughly, he shoved Dominic aside and leaned into the stove to lift out the wood Dominic had carefully arranged. Snickering, the rest of the group crept into the classroom, their arms full of stones, snow, and trash. As Dominic bit his lip angrily, they dumped these into the stove then slammed the door shut.

"Not a bad job, eh, Savio?" Di Marzio commented mischievously, grabbing the lad's wrist. "C'mon, you're coming with us to finish that snowball fight."

It took all Dominic had not to lash out at them. Silently, he returned with them outside, knowing he could not get them to undo the low prank they had played.

All morning long, the boys shivered at their lessons. Dominic's fingers were so numb he could scarcely keep them closed over his pen. Thrusting up a sideward glance, he noticed that the hands of the student next to him were blue. Angelo was shaking like a leaf in front of him, his teeth noisily chattering.

"Argh, I can't focus!" muttered an exasperated boy behind him.

"What's that, Picasa?" Father Cugliero inquired.

"Nothing, Father."

"Very well. As I was saying, we form the present subjunctive verb in Latin by removing the signature vowel from the second principal part of the verb and replacing it with one of the following vowels, depending on the verb's conjugation. When dealing with a first conjugation verb, we remove the 'a' and replace it with an 'e' —."

Dominic struggled to follow, hastily scribbling down notes as the priest scratched an explanation on the board. His icy fingers couldn't go fast enough.

"For a second conjugation verb —." Father Cugliero suddenly threw down his chalk and spun around to face the class. "All right, what's going on? Something's wrong." A room full of surprised and innocent faces looked back at him. "All morning long you've been fidgeting and wriggling — more than usual, I should add. What is it?"

"Nothing's wrong, Father," someone volunteered, "'cept it's awfully cold in here."

Father Cugliero realized he did feel quite cold. Somewhat vexed, he strode over to the stove and touched it quickly with his fingertips. Then he laid his hand flat on the lid. It was cold. Throwing open the door, he peered inside. Not a flame greeted him, but a pile of rocks, rubbish, and snow!

"Who did this?" he thundered.

A class of guiltless faces stared at him. Some of them looked angry that someone had played such a nasty trick.

"This was done on purpose," Father Cugliero growled, searching their faces one by one. "Snow and rocks and old garbage don't magically appear in stoves. Who did it?"

Just then the clock struck twelve for the Angelus and lunch. The indignant priest struggled to compose himself for the midday prayers; when these were over, he turned again to the class.

"This was a very heartless prank, and I expect that whoever did it will own up during the lunch period. You may be dismissed."

The boys trooped out in subdued silence, knowing that such an act deserved expulsion. It could very well be that one of their classmates would not return tomorrow.

Father Cugliero watched them leave with cold sternness. Once the last had gone, he slumped into his chair and covered his face with his hands. Who could have stooped to such a mean trick? No wonder the boys hadn't been able to focus. They had been freezing cold. How hard and cruel could a youngster get?

Half the lunch break passed, and no one came to confess. Father Cugliero felt increasingly depressed. So the culprit didn't even have the moral integrity to own up. Sighing, he left the classroom to fetch a glass of water.

It was in the hallway that he found them, whispering and gesturing anxiously. As soon as they saw him, they hushed each other and looked at him with sorrowful, disappointed eyes. The same old group of mischief-makers. He could have guessed as much.

Expecting an avowal of guilt, Father Cugliero snapped, "Well? What is it? Was it you?"

"Oh, no, Father!" Antonio Di Marzio cried, his voice full of sincerity. "We wanted to tell you about it, but it certainly wasn't any of us!"

Father Cugliero glared at them. Just who else in this school would have done it, he thought suspiciously, but he held his tongue. The boys glanced at each other uneasily, as if loathe to continue.

"Well?" the priest demanded impatiently. "Go on, and don't waste my time."

"It was Savio, Father!" Di Marzio blurted out. "Dominic Savio! We saw him do it!"

"Dominic Savio!" Father Cugliero roared. "Get out of my sight, you liars! Of all the people in the world, Savio would be the very last –!"

"Please, Father, hear us out!" Di Marzio begged. "We know no one'd expect such a thing from him, and we wouldn't have believed it ourselves if we hadn't seen it! But we saw the whole thing happen. Someone chucked a snowball at him as he was bringing in wood, and he got all mad because the wood got wet. You know how it was his turn to fix up the stove this morning..."

Father Cugliero paused, his heart going cold. No! – not Savio! *Not* Savio! But bit by bit, as Di Marzio suavely spoke on, he realized that what he heard had to be the truth. It struck him like an aching blow. Savio, Dominic Savio! – of all people! It hurt too much to comprehend – of all the devout, good-natured boys he had taught, he had never known any better – of all the kind, honest, studious – it was too much!

Overwhelmed by piercing disappointment, Father Cugliero rushed back into the classroom, his dismay turning into white anger at having been so deceived.

The class was back in their seats by now. Eyes blazing, he shouted out, "I've discovered the culprit, and I'm thoroughly ashamed of you! To have kept the whole class in a freezing condition for a whole morning is utterly cruel and base and deserves immediate expulsion! I can't even imagine that any of you would have dreamt of doing this, and then to not even admit it!" He turned on Dominic in a rage. "And you had to be the one to do this!"

The class gasped. Not Savio – their friend and hero! – it couldn't be!

At that point, Di Marzio and his friends slipped into the room, and Dominic instantly understood what had happened. His mind retreated into nimble calculations.

"Don't you know you should be expelled for this?" Father Cugliero's voice was rolling over him like thunder. "You're lucky it's your first offense. Make sure it's your last!"

Dominic hardly heard him. One thing was clear in his mind. He must keep silent. The whole class was staring at him, waiting, hoping, wordlessly pleading for him to assert his innocence and restore his honor; the words burned on his tongue, and the injustice flamed in his eyes – only a few words, and both class and teacher would believe him – but he could not speak; Di Marzio was on his last chance – Christ, too, had remained silent...

And with fierce depths of manly courage and heavenly grace, Dominic Savio bowed his head in admission of the guilt, lowered his eyes so as not to betray his emotion, and spoke not a word.

Angelo shuffled his feet dismally on the way to school. One of his books dropped into the snow, and he picked it up mechanically, hardly caring that the pages were wet. Oh, how could it be true? His old buddy Dominic, who had always been so good and kind – what could have gotten into him? But no, Angelo told himself defiantly, he'd never believe it! It couldn't possibly have been Dominic! But then why hadn't he said anything?

Angelo kicked a pebble disconsolately and scowled as it bounced off the road. The whole school was in a turmoil. We thought he was our noble friend, not a mean prankster. We all looked up to him...until now. We thought that was the best a fellow could get; he inspired us so much — now it's hard to believe really good kids exist. We wanted to be like him, but if that's what being good is like, we don't care for it anymore. And most of all: how could Savio, of all people, have done that?

They felt betrayed. But Angelo wasn't so sure. He had known Dominic much longer than the rest of them had. He knew well that while Dominic sometimes did things that were a little strange, he vigorously fought against anything that was wrong. No, no — Dominic might talk to his guardian angel on the way to school and do other such crazy things, but he wouldn't play a heartless trick on his companions. Not the Dominic he knew. But supposing...Angelo's heart skipped a beat. Supposing he had changed during his year at Castelnuovo? Supposing he had only pretended to be good so he would be liked at his new school here in Mondonio?

Yet the strange part was that Dominic was the same happy, energetic — yes, and considerate — friend he had always been. It really didn't seem that any heavy guilt was eating at his conscience. Even the fact that many of his old friends had turned a cold shoulder on him didn't seem to bother him much. *Did* it bother him? Maybe he was just hiding it. After all, he'd always been a rather sensitive fellow. But if he *was* hiding it, he was doing a remarkable job.

Dejectedly, Angelo entered the schoolyard and found Dominic whole-heartedly chasing a handful of boys. When he saw his friend, he stopped, his face flushed and smiling.

"Morning, Angelo! Give you three before I'm after you! One —!"

"Can't, Dom. I need to finish learning my lessons."

"Aw, that's too bad. Want any help?"

"That's all right. I don't have much left."

What was wrong with him? he thought furiously. Any other day he would have gladly accepted Dominic's help. After yesterday, however — but no, he would never believe Dominic had done it! Except...

Miserably, he went into the school and curled up on the floor in the hallway. He opened his book and began to read, but not a word was processed in his mind. He was about to give up when he heard voices around the corner of the hall.

"Not a shabby job, Di Marzio," a familiar voice remarked complacently. "Quite the con artist you are."

"I didn't think he'd believe you, but you sure pulled it off nice!"

"Yeah, you sly old cat, no one else could've put the blame on Savio like that 'cept you."

Angelo went white. Dominic was innocent! His pulse beat at breakneck speed, and he felt like yelling at it to shut up. They couldn't find him — if they did, he was done for — he held his breath until he thought he'd burst, as they talked on casually.

"No one says a word of this, you hear?" Di Marzio was warning dangerously. "Anyone who does is good as dead. I'll get expelled if anyone finds out I did it."

Angelo's eyes went round like saucers. *They* had done it. Of course, they had! And they were going to kill him because — he clenched his fists and gritted his teeth — because he *was* going to tell Father Cugliero, no matter what they did to him. He imagined Di Marzio leaning over him with a knife but desperately shut his mind against it. No, he would tell Father — not for the world would he keep Dominic in undeserved shame! Forcing himself to remain calm, he squeezed his eyes shut in heroic resolve. That time the boys had bullied Dominic about the apricots, he had told him that next time he'd take the beating with him. Well, that beating was right around the corner.

He stood up and started running toward Father Cugliero's classroom as fast as his legs could carry him.

"Hey, Dom! Father wants you."

Dominic stopped short on the verge of tagging someone and found Angelo beckoning to him. To his horror, Angelo's face was puffed up with bruises.

"Goodness! What happened to you? Those lessons really gave it to you, I see!"

Angelo attempted a grin which turned into a wince of pain. "Got caught telling tales," he answered briefly.

"You telling –!"

Dominic suddenly halted and looked at him keenly. Without another word, he tossed a grateful arm around Angelo's shoulder, as they walked into the school and down the hallway. At the door of Father Cugliero's classroom, Dominic paused and smiled impishly.

"No apricots, I guess?"

Angelo laughed and felt that all the apricots in the world couldn't match the reward of having helped his friend.

Inside the classroom, Dominic found his teacher buried behind a mound of books and papers. Father Cugliero gave him a searching look when he entered.

"I've discovered the real culprits, Dominic," he said. His voice was a little choked up, to the boy's surprise. "Why didn't you say anything?"

Dominic reddened and shifted his feet uncomfortably. "Well, Father, I knew that boy would have been expelled if you found out he'd done it, and I thought maybe you'd let me off." He hung his head and added, almost in a whisper, "Besides, Our Lord was falsely accused, too, and He didn't say anything."

For a few moments, Father Cugliero had to cover his face to hide his overwhelming emotion. When he looked up, his eyes were red.

"I'm sorry I scolded you unjustly, son. That's all. You may go."

"One more thing, Father?" Dominic began hesitantly.

"Yes?"

"Will you let Di Marzio stay?"

The priest gave him a blank stare. Dominic put on his most winning smile.

"Since you asked," Father Cugliero relented at last. "I'll give him one last chance." His face broke into a grin. "Now out with you, before you convince me to let him stay for the rest of his life!"

Dominic laughed merrily and scooted out of the room, his face lit with happiness.

"Here," thought the priest in amazement, as he watched Dominic leave, "is an innocent soul in whom Heaven takes delight and who in his heart's desire already lives with the angels."

———————

"Thanks for helping me out today, Angelo," Dominic said as the two boys walked home from school. "It was you, wasn't it?"

"Don't bother about it. I'd do anything for you, Dom."

Gently, Dominic studied Angelo's bruises and answered, "It seems you would."

They continued in silence for a while until suddenly Angelo asked, "How come you're so good, Dom? You...you make me wanna lead a good life, but I get stuck over things like fighting with my brothers, or...or...I don't know. What makes you so holy? I never could've kept quiet about Di Marzio like that."

"Whenever I've done good it's because Our Lady helped me,"

Dominic answered seriously. "She's always ready to help us, Angelo."

"I guess you're right. Only I don't know why she'd care much for a dud like me. It's not as if I'm another Saint Ignatius."

Dominic meditated a moment. "She doesn't think like that," he finally asserted. "She wasn't a Saint Ignatius during her life, either, you know. Just a quiet and wonderful mother. She doesn't mind if a soul is little, because she was that way herself. In fact, she loves the little souls like you and me, because we need her help terribly, and she loves to help us."

Angelo cocked a wondering eyebrow at his friend. "Say, Dom, how'd you know all that?"

"Talk to her," Dominic grinned. "You'll find out for yourself." He gazed out into the distance where the blue hills melted into the sky, and a burning light of passion drifted into his eyes. "I need to bring souls to her, so she can save them," he said in a low, resolute voice. "If only I could go to the Oratory!"

Angelo furrowed his brows. Dominic had told him of this desire before, but Angelo was confused. Everyone knew about Don Bosco, the miracle-worker and saint of Turin, and about his famous Oratory for boys; but Angelo had always thought the Oratory was a home for poor, crime-committing orphan kids Don Bosco picked off the streets. Not for country boys with good, strong families.

"Why'd you want to go to the Oratory?" he demanded aloud. "Aren't half the fellows in there from jail?"

Dominic laughed heartily. "Maybe some of them are. What, are you scared they'd murder me? But I don't think they're going back to jail after being at the Oratory." His face grew grave. "I want to go to the Oratory so I can become a priest and save souls. So many people need our help, Angelo."

There was a fierce gaze of longing in his eyes, and when Angelo saw it, some of its fire seemed to leap into his own soul and set a sweet, intense pain blazing through his chest. People did need help, so much help. Why shouldn't he be the one to give it? But then, just look at Dominic, so on fire with holiness! How could he, Angelo, be of any help to anyone when he was the very one who needed help? No, people like Dominic could be saints, but Angelo wasn't ready. In fact, he'd probably never be ready. He could never be like Dominic.

Poor little Angelo, don't you realize that sainthood is for now and is different for each of us? That was the secret Dominic knew.

"I promise you, Don Bosco, you may have dozens of holy boys here at your Oratory, but not one is better than Dominic Savio." Father Cugliero banged his fist emphatically on the rough wooden table. "He's another Saint Aloysius Gonzaga, and I wouldn't say that about anyone, you know."

"No, you wouldn't," Don Bosco agreed. A smile tugged at the corners of his mouth, partly because he was amused at the other's fervor and partly because his heart thrilled to hear any traces of holiness in a young person.

"Exactly. I wouldn't," Father Cugliero repeated. "When he prays, he really *prays*, and with his classmates he's thoughtful and energetic and just everything they could ask for! They all love him, Don Bosco, and for a boy to be devout like that and still admired by his less devout companions is no small feat, as I'm sure you know."

"That's true. It shows he has no haughtiness mixed up in his devotion."

"None at all."

"He plays hard, you say?" Don Bosco knew the necessity of a well-balanced life.

"Harder than he should." Father Cugliero shook his head. "He's not very strong, but the way he plays those games you'd think his life depended on it."

Don Bosco laughed. "I like it, I like it! And he wants to be a priest, eh?"

"Yes, he's mentioned it to me a couple times. That's why I think he'd do well to go to your Oratory. Here he could get the education he needs as well as the spiritual formation you'd give him."

"Tell you what," Don Bosco decided, "I'll be visiting Murialdo with my boys for the Feast of the Holy Rosary. What about sending him over to see me then?"

"There's about to be an explosion," Father Cugliero thought on his way home. "Dominic's the fire and Don Bosco's the gasoline. Everyone around them better look out."

———————

Dominic lay on one side, listening to the crickets. How he was going to get through this night he had no idea. Restlessly, he turned to his other side. Maybe if he shut his eyes...nope, that wasn't working. Don Bosco...

He had heard so many things about the famous priest – how he had been a poor country boy like Dominic himself, how he had longed to be a priest and despite his extreme poverty had struggled his way into becoming one. That in itself was enough for Dominic to feel a deep connection to him. But then there were so many other things that should almost be alarming if you stopped to think about them: how he could read souls and cure the sick, how he had seen visions and had had prophetic dreams, how he had a mysterious dog that protected him in dangerous parts of town but was never seen otherwise – yes, rather an intimidating kind of person to be meeting with tomorrow, but was he intimidated? No, not really, just...he couldn't place his finger on it. He had no idea what he was feeling; he only knew that he was meeting Don Bosco tomorrow, and perhaps this extraordinary person would take him to the Oratory where he so longed to go.

But that would mean leaving his family, and Dominic would miss them terribly. He wouldn't be there when chubby little Guglielmo learned to talk or when Giovanni had his first day of school — why, they would grow up hardly knowing him! And as much as Raimonda and Maria got on his nerves sometimes, he couldn't imagine living without them. They had had so much fun together; to think that was perhaps at an end was almost too much to bear.

And yet...something in his heart leapt with electric hope at the thought of living at the Oratory. There at last he would be free to become a priest; there he would be in the presence of a saint; there he would find companions who would teach him to love Jesus better and companions whose souls he would make it his mission to chase into the Heart of Christ. He knew the Oratory was a holy place, and he ardently wanted to be holy. No, he didn't merely want to become holy; he needed to become holy.

It was a long night before he finally fell asleep.

The morning of October 2, 1854 dawned with golden radiance over the peaceful village of Mondonio. Dominic and his father set out early for Murialdo.

If Dominic felt any nervousness, it melted away the moment he laid eyes on Don Bosco. The soul of a saint felt the presence of a saint and responded accordingly; that is, with full confidence and intimate understanding.

"What's your name, son?"

"Dominic Savio, Father, from Mondonio. I'm the boy Father Cugliero told you about."

"It's good to meet you, Dominic! How about we walk a bit and you tell me about your studies?"

They walked side by side, Don Bosco asking questions and Dominic giving his sincere answers.

Although he was often shy with strangers, Dominic soon found himself opening the innermost doors of his heart to the priest in complete ease. Don Bosco, too, writes of the instant kinship he felt with the other: "something in his demeanor fixed my attention upon him...and we were immediately on the most friendly and confidential terms. I may say that I at once recognized a boy after God's own heart."

On a sprawling field dotted with glorious autumn trees, a crowd of boys from the Oratory were romping and yelling with zealous vivacity. Dominic watched them with a smile. How he'd love to join them at the Oratory! He felt he was close to dying of suspense, so, practically, he asked the question burning on his mind.

"Well, Father? Do you think you'll let me come to the Oratory?"

Don Bosco smiled at his directness. "I think I see very good material to work on."

Dominic at once comprehended his meaning. "Material to make what?"

"Something beautiful for Our Lord."

"I see! I'm the material and you're going to fashion me."

The two hearts glowed.

"Exactly, son."

"You'll take me with you then, won't you?" Dominic couldn't restrain the longing in his voice.

"I want to, except..." Don Bosco's voice trailed off, as the boy's eyes hung on his face in searching anxiety. "Well, you're not very strong, Dominic, and the studying may wear you down."

There was an audible sigh of relief as Dominic's face lit up into its old easy smile. "Oh, don't worry about that, Father! God's always given me the strength I needed, and I know He always will."

Once again Don Bosco felt deeply moved.

"What do you want to do after you finish your studies?" he inquired.

Dominic shone. "If I can hope for such a favor from God," he replied, "I ardently desire to become a priest."

This was one of the most stirring and clear characteristics of Dominic's life; that if he wanted something, he wanted it intensely and would take on any obstacle to attain it. Yet he patterned his desires after the Will of God, and this fierce tenacity, combined with the guiding finger of God, was the reason he soared to the Heart of the Divine in so short a time. Thus it was that it was never enough for him to be merely religious; he must be a saint. It was not enough for him to reach heaven; his classmates must come with him — all of them. It was not enough for him to avoid impurity; he would die before committing it.

Don Bosco gazed into his earnest face and knew it was a priceless gem God was entrusting to him. Thoughtfully, he drew out a copy of his *Catholic Readings* and handed it to the youth.

"Take this and see if you can learn the first page by tomorrow. I'm going to talk over some things with your dad. You can run outside and play with the other boys in the meantime."

Ten minutes later, Dominic reappeared and handed the book to Don Bosco. "I'm ready, Father."

"What! I wanted you to memorize it!"

"I know." He launched into a perfect recital of the page, then went on to explain the lesson with astonishing clarity and comprehension.

Don Bosco stared, hardly believing his ears.

"Well done!" he nearly choked, when Dominic had finished. "Since you've anticipated your lesson, I'll anticipate my answer." He rested an affectionate smile on the boy's eager face. "Yes, Dominic, you may come to the Oratory. Beg the good God to help both you and me do His Holy Will."

Dominic felt a rush of deep, sweet joy, as his blue eyes sparkled with gratitude. Unable to speak, he seized the priest's hand and kissed it reverently. At last he found voice enough to whisper, "I hope I never give you reason to complain."

Then a huge grin lighted over his face, and darting off, he threw himself exuberantly into the crowd of boys.

The explosion had begun.

Three

Dominic squeezed his little brother Guglielmo in a crushing hug.

"You'll make him throw up his breakfast," Maria accused him.

He winked at her mischievously. "That's all right! You'll clean him up."

She started after him with a shove which ended up in another hug bathed in tears.

"I'll miss you, Dom."

"Aw, don't worry. I'll be back. Can't get rid of me that easily, sorry for you."

She finished the shove, and he fell back laughing.

It was a difficult morning for Dominic, though he bravely tried to hide his sorrow. As much as he wanted to live at the Oratory, he could scarcely tear himself away from his family. One comfort was that Don Bosco had recruited Angelo, too, despite the latter's terror of juvenile delinquents. Glancing around the room at the familiar faces and objects, he felt an aching lump swell up in his throat and swallowed it hard. Don't cry...don't cry...his eyes met those of his stricken mother, and he almost lost control of himself completely.

"There, there," she sobbed, "don't mind me. Be a good boy, Dominic, as you've always been, and I won't have any reason to cry. It's just that –."

She burst into fresh tears and held him tightly in her arms.

When his last glimpse of home melted beyond the hills, he let his tears creep out at last. The well-known fields, fences, and cottages slipped gently away, and he watched them disappear into his past through blurred eyes. Sometimes God's Will is hard.

But when they reached the city, alive and roaring with its vendors, street urchins, soldiers, and government officials, some of his homesickness gave way to curiosity. He marveled at the enormous stone buildings and towering church steeples and watched as ragged boys chased each other between carriages drawn by stomping horses. Everywhere he looked there was motion, so unlike his tranquil Mondonio. Despite the rawness in his heart, he felt a thrill of anticipation course through his veins. There would be so much excitement living here in Turin.

At last they arrived at the Oratory. The sight that greeted him was a horde of boys hollering and running joyously about in front of a long, shabby building. Dominic took one look and stepped through the gates with a grin. He felt perfectly at home.

A buoyant, welcoming fellow took Dominic and his father to Don Bosco's office. He looked about sixteen, with a pair of dark, roguish eyes and a quick dimple that told of a rash and vivacious spirit.

"Name's Giovanni Cagliero." He held out his hand and Dominic shook it warmly. "Yours?"

"Dominic Savio."

Their eyes met frankly; both identified a generous and noble heart in the other; and a friendship was established that would last until death.

"It's good to have you! And this is your dad?"

"Yes."

"Nice to meet you, Signor. I'll show you both to Don Bosco." He turned to Dominic as they walked into the building. "Will you be studying or working as an apprentice?"

"Studying. What do you do?"

"Study, too. We don't do it here, though. There are too many of us. Don Bosco knows teachers around Turin who teach us for free, and we join their classes."

"How do you like the Oratory?"

A quick smile flashed over the lad's honest face. "I love it. We all do. 'Cept the troublemakers, but when they get to be good, they love it, too."

Dominic laughed outright at his confident generalization. "All the troublemakers get to be good?"

"Most of them. You usually can't help it around here." He threw Dominic a sidelong grin. "I'd know."

"Oh, really?" Dominic felt a surge of delighted interest.

"Uh-huh. I used to run off on the way back from school and pick up tricks from the street performers and then run back as fast as these legs could move. I got the timing so well I'd get back to the Oratory just when everyone else did. One of the seminarians, named Michael Rua, almost had me kicked out of the Oratory. He's good and holy but just strict. Anyway, we're friends now, and Don Bosco won me over eventually. He knows a boy's heart inside out, I'll tell you that."

Dominic's last shreds of shyness about the Oratory vanished into thin air. When he entered Don Bosco's office, it was with a huge smile on his young face.

"Hello, Dominic!" the priest cried. "Here at last! And welcome, Signor Savio. How are things in Mondonio?"

As his father and Don Bosco chatted a while, Dominic glanced around the room. He immediately noticed that it was poorly furnished, just like the rest of the Oratory. A rickety bookshelf stood against the wall, and a scratched-up desk was placed in the middle of the room. There was a kneeler in the corner, worn, faded, and clearly well-loved. Up on the wall hung a sign written in Latin. Dominic scrunched his forehead in thought. *Da mihi animas*...well, *mihi* was *to me*, and *animas* was *soul* – no, *souls* –.

"What are you looking at?" Don Bosco broke into his thoughts.

"That sign."

"Ah. Hit upon the target already, I see. Can you read it?"

"I'm not sure. *Da...*"

"From *dare*," Don Bosco hinted.

"Oh, *to give*! That makes sense, then. *Give me souls*!" He read on. "*Caetera tolle*. Gee, that's a mouthful, Father. I'm not so sure."

"It is a mouthful, isn't it?" Don Bosco's eyes twinkled. "*Caetera* means *the rest*, and *tolle* means *take away*. *Give me souls; take away the rest*. See?"

Dominic nodded and looked thoughtfully at the sign for a moment. "I think I understand, Don Bosco. Here the goal isn't to get money but to win souls." A gentle light entered his countenance. "I hope my soul is one of them."

––––––––––

"Giovanni Cagliero, Giovanni Massaglia, Angelo Savio, Dominic

Savio." A sturdy, brown-haired boy, the said Giovanni Massaglia, looked at Dominic and grinned. "I vote we call ourselves the Giovanni Savios."

"Hey, Massaglia, that's a good one!" Cagliero hollered, clapping his friend vigorously on the back. "Now I say it's time for the Giovannis to get the Savios on their feet around here. No running off with the blankets from *our* charges, eh?" He nudged Angelo. "Someone did that once. Wasn't me."

"All right, all right, we'll start by running to the chapel," Massaglia declared. "Ready, set —."

"Hey, the Savios don't know where that is!" Dominic protested.

"Aw, you weren't supposed to think of that. I would've beat you. All right, then, the Giovannis will race to the chapel, and you Savios can chase us to make us go faster. Go!"

They took off and reached the chapel out of breath.

"This is," Cagliero panted, "Saint Francis de Sales Church. Mass at 6:30. I beat you, Massaglia."

"In your dreams. Let's go in."

Dominic thrust a swift glance at Massaglia as they took off their caps and walked into the church. His mother had always taught him to be good and friendly to everyone he met but only to be good friends with those of noble character. It seemed to him that Cagliero and Massaglia would be two staunch friends, and his soul warmed to the thought. A happy smile on his lips, he knelt down and crossed himself.

O Jesus! He felt his heart would burst for joy. *Here at the Oratory at last! How good You are, dearest Lord! How can I ever thank You? You've done so, so much for me, and I'm such a wreck in return. Help me love You, Jesus, especially here at the Oratory — oh, Lord! I want to love You! Help me, Jesus, or I can do nothing. You alone can make me a saint. Mamma, help me...*

He heard the other boys getting up from the pew and looked up to find Massaglia's eyes resting on him intently. They smiled at each other and left the church.

"Next you meet Mamma Margaret," Cagliero announced. "Don Bosco's mother. She'll give you a spoon."

"What for?" a baffled Angelo demanded.

"Eating," Cagliero replied gravely. "You use it to scoop your soup into your mouth."

"Aw, let him be!" Massaglia flew to the rescue of a red-faced but laughing Angelo. "We take care of our own utensils," he explained. "If you don't want them to get stolen, keep them in your pockets."

Within a few efficient minutes, Cagliero and Massaglia had shown the two new boys their dorms, given them a quick tour of the grounds, and explained all the basic rules of the Oratory.

"We try to serve God as best we can here," Massaglia said. "And to help us do that, Don Bosco encourages us to go to Confession and Communion often." He hesitated, watching their faces. "I know some fellows don't care much for the Sacraments, but they really help a lot, you know."

Dominic was smiling. This was the kind of person Massaglia was. This was the kind of company he was in!

"I know," he answered, and Massaglia met his eyes and grinned broadly.

"We're supposed to go to daily Mass," Cagliero continued, "and you won't exactly get in trouble if you don't, but just do it. Whenever I go a day without Mass, I feel the same way as when I'm trying to kick a badly deflated football."

The boys burst out laughing, and Dominic elbowed Angelo.

"Some jailbirds, huh?" he whispered mischievously.

Angelo only laughed harder and shook his head.

It didn't take Dominic long to realize that some of the Oratory boys really could have come from jail as Angelo had once suggested. Not everyone was as zealous and generous-hearted as Cagliero and Massaglia; in fact, several were violent, unruly, and scornful of religion. But neither did it take him long to discover that the Oratory was holy ground, and many of the young souls there were turned wholly to God, open and ready to follow Him. Cagliero and Massaglia were not the only ones. There was Bonetti and Marcellino and Rua and Bongiovanni and so many others — souls so ardently seeking their Maker yet so normal in their everyday classes and games that Dominic found himself perpetually edified just by watching them.

Then there was Don Bosco himself. Each day Dominic's love and admiration for the saintly priest grew, in observing him say Mass, in listening to his homilies and evening talks, in speaking with him, and in witnessing his profound devotion to his boys. Just to see Don Bosco made a person pause and remember Jesus Christ. Yet he, too, like the boys he had formed, combined a normal, human mannerism with his deep, pulsating holiness. Sainthood never once robbed anyone of a good, honest laugh. Thus it was that the boys flocked to him, treasured his advice, and struggled to be like him. He made holiness not just attractive to them, but something they craved with all the bursting energy of their youthful hearts. Here was someone who understood them; who laughed with them and ate with them; who wept, prayed, and sacrificed for them; who spent every penny and every minute providing for them yet was wholly present if any one of them needed to unburden his heart — of course they loved him. Of course they yearned to be like him. Not to say they never gave him trouble, but those who caught sight of his goal caught hands and ran with each other in his colossal footsteps. If their beloved Don Bosco was going to heaven, they were going there, too.

Dominic caught the spirit in no time at all. To a soul already attuned to God's voice, the Oratory was balm, fuel, and battleground all in one. There he was challenged, but more than anything, there he was lifted by God in one soaring ascent to the height of Love. There he fought, and there his battles were won. It was at the Oratory that Dominic Savio's crown of sainthood was forged.

Yet at first he was much like the other devout boys: scrupulous in following the rules and learning his lessons, exemplary and good-natured in and out of class, attentive in prayer, and respectful to peers and superiors alike. The boys took to him and he to them, but they found nothing strikingly unusual about him. Perhaps he was waiting to win their hearts and confidence before letting loose his tiger of zeal. Or — and considering his all-or-nothing nature, this is more likely — perhaps it was Our Lady who was sharpening her knight's sword with the blade of time before sending him flying into the offensive.

Whichever it was, his first month at the Oratory was quiet but remarkably formative. During the homilies, in class, and at Don Bosco's evening talks to his boys, Dominic devoured any instruction regarding the living of his Faith with voracious eagerness. Any advice to further him in the path of virtue he pondered and stored in his memory, like Mary, who treasured the Word of God in her heart and contemplated it continually. And the questions he asked! Again and again, Don Bosco found the puzzled face appearing at his door or his elbow with a question about something he had just taught.

"I've been thinking about what you said the other day, Father, but I just don't understand..."

Don Bosco would twist away a smile and explain the answers to Dominic's questions. Within a few minutes, the light would dawn over the boy's brow, and with happy thanks, he would run off to join his companions.

Mamma Margaret, Don Bosco's mother, noticed the boy's devotion very quickly.

"You'd better keep an eye on that one," she told her son, after one of Dominic's questions had been answered.

"Oh?"

The good woman watched Dominic dash into a crowd of boys with motherly affection shining in her eyes.

"Yes, Giovanni. He prays like an angel and always seems to have his mind on God. Say what you like, he'll outstrip the best of your boys."

"Now, Mamma, holiness isn't a competition," Don Bosco teased her.

"I'm not saying it is, I'm just saying he'll outdo them."

Don Bosco put on a pretense of doubt, and Mamma Margaret snorted and flicked her dishwater at him. "Trust me, Giovanni Bosco," she said. "Something's about to happen."

———————

The church was full of boys. Dominic struggled to concentrate on the Mass, but his eyes kept drifting off to the faces around him. There were sixty-five boarders at the Oratory, and already he knew most of them. It was so exciting to meet them all, to find friends who understood and shared his likes and dislikes, his character traits, his ideals, and most of all his love for Christ. Many of his new acquaintances couldn't have cared less for that last, but that didn't stop him from liking them, and they gladly returned the comradeship. Only a month had passed by, yet he fit right in with these boys as if he had been living here his whole life.

A certain face stuck out to him, both distracting him from the prayers and inspiring him, and that was Massaglia's. Reverent, focused, and peaceful, it revealed a soul thrust deeply into prayer, and it drew Dominic's attention like a magnet. There, he knew beyond doubt, knelt a true friend who would pull him up towards heaven with undying perseverance. He had seen Massaglia in prayer and had noticed the genuine, respectful air he bore to others, but that wasn't all. A soul seeking God can quickly identify that same whole-hearted search in another, and Dominic identified this distinctly in Massaglia. Since they had met each other, they had exchanged warm smiles in passing and had spoken a few times, but what Dominic wanted was an explicit avowal of shared core values. He wanted friendship to grow from those values and those values to grow from their friendship.

Of course, as a twelve-and-a-half-year-old, he wasn't thinking these things exactly. He was more thinking in exasperation that if the sight of someone praying could distract him from his own prayers so easily, then there must be something seriously wrong with him. But etched in his unconscious thoughts, in his unnoticed and unanalyzed feelings, he knew these things — that such a friendship would be a jewel and that he wanted it. He believed it so unshakably that he didn't have to think it.

When Mass was over, the boys filed out of the church, leaving a few of their companions behind to pray in solitude. Needless to say, two of these were Dominic and Massaglia. The former covered his face with his hands and hurled himself into honest contrition for having paid so little attention in Mass.

Never again, Jesus! I mean, I'll try... Never again if You give me lots and lots and lots of help. Next time I'll sit in front of Massaglia. O Jesus! Help me realize just what the Mass is! If only I truly understood, I wouldn't even be able to get distracted. Sweet Mother, help me see!

At last he aroused himself. When he reached the back of the church, he found Massaglia waiting for him. They grinned and walked out together, hastened by the aroma of Mamma Margaret's breakfast cooking.

"What's up, Savio?"

"Just thinking, you seem to pray pretty hard. Do you ever get distracted?"

"Oh, sure. Lots of times. But Don Bosco says to receive every Communion as if it were our last, and that helps me focus."

"Smart man, that Don Bosco! I'll do that from now on."

"I always thought you prayed super hard already."

"Not hard enough," Dominic sighed earnestly. "I just want to love Him, *really* love Him, you know what I mean?"

"Yes," Massaglia answered. "Make Him the utter focus of your life."

"Exactly. There are so many things to say and learn and do, and I end up forgetting Him so easily. I want to be thinking about Him every moment of the day, like Mary, and especially during Mass."

"Oh, I know just how you feel! It seems pretty lousy of us to be thinking of anything other than the One Who made us, saved us, and has a pressing and important mission for us." He glanced at Dominic as if measuring up his trustworthiness, then added, "I want to be a priest someday and remind people of these things, but I don't feel worthy at all."

Dominic's face lit up. "Hey, Massaglia, that's wonderful! I want to be a priest, too! It's true though, I don't feel worthy either. I don't see how anyone ever could. But it's not enough for us to just want the priesthood, you know. We've got to prepare ourselves for it by growing in virtue."

"I'm fully aware of it. And I know if God is calling us to this, He'll give us all the graces we need. But it's still mind-blowing to think about."

Chords were touched in Dominic's soul with every sentence Massaglia uttered. Little did he know his friend felt the same way.

Thus were the two souls bonded, in pure and enduring friendship. Not a day would pass that they did not encourage and edify each other, sometimes in long conversation or prayer, but often in merely a heartening smile or by gentle example. It was a short journey they traveled together, but urged on by one another's guidance, they went towards their Maker with staunch sureness and incredible speed.

———

"Don Bosco, would you do me a favor?"

"What is it, Dominic?"

"Would you tell me when you see faults I have, so I can fix them?"

"I'll gladly help you that way."

"Thanks, Father! Also, I want to do something special for the Feast of the Immaculate Conception."

"Of course!" Don Bosco agreed. "What do you have in mind? A novena, maybe?"

Dominic smiled abashedly. "Well, I'm already doing that. And to tell you the truth, each day of the novena has been filling me with so much love for Our Lady that I feel as if I'll burst pretty soon. I need to do something more."

Don Bosco tenderly searched the boy's face. He had indeed noticed a swift flight in Dominic's ardor over the past few days. Each day it was stronger, fiercer, deeper. "How about receiving Communion frequently? Nothing delights Our Lady more than a devout reception of her Son."

"I receive Him every week already. There's something more I want to do, if you'll give me permission."

"Which is?"

"I want to make a general confession and then," his face took on a radiant glow, "I want to consecrate myself completely to Mary. You see, Don Bosco, I'd rather die than commit a mortal sin, but I know how easily I can fall, even despite my longing to remain pure. So I need her help. She's entirely spotless, and I know she'll keep me safe."

What solace to the soul of the priest who spent his life battling for the purity of his youthful charges, only to see them stray again and again into the clutches of sin! As Dominic clung to this sweet angelic virtue at all costs, so too did Don Bosco, and his student's simple but heartfelt words filled him with consolation.

"Of course you may, Dominic. God bless you."

That year, Pope Pius IX was proclaiming the dogma of the Immaculate Conception, that Mary had been conceived without Original Sin. Catholics had always known that the Mother of God is entirely without sin (for what son who could create his own mother would make her anything but perfect?), but now it was being formally proclaimed as dogma. To Dominic, the fierce guardian of purity, such a clear and powerful statement of his dearest Mother's sinlessness held tremendous significance. To him who prayed each day "Death before sin!" was now being announced in the full solemnity of papal infallibility that there was one – Mary, Dominic's gentle Mother – who had lived his motto to the utmost degree. How could he pass such a day without entrusting himself, his salvation, and his purity to her care?

The great day dawned over a mantle of snow, December 8, 1854, a day forever sealed in the Church's memory as one of great rejoicing. After Mass had ended, Dominic crept to the statue of the Virgin Mary, trembling slightly with emotion. His eyes blazed with a love that seemed almost too intense to be confined in his fragile body, as he knelt down and thrust himself into throbbing, fervent prayer.

Everything is yours, my sweetest Mother. My soul, my body, my possessions, every thought, word, act – all for you. Take me, all of me, and bring me to Jesus. Let me love Him as you do and love you as He does...make me perfect, for Him...

Thus flowed his prayer, cried out from the depths of a heart consumed in Divine fire. Mary heard and rushed to him. Rapturously, she accepted his humble gift of himself and instantly set to work forming a masterpiece. And from then on, Dominic Savio was transformed.

At last he blinked his eyes open and in a daze, drew out from his pocket a worn slip of paper. Unfolding it, he whispered the words written there in a young, unsteady hand. Many, many a time had he repledged these words, the guiding promises of his life.

Resolutions made by me, Dominic Savio, in the year 1849, on the day of my First Communion, at the age of seven.

1. *I will go to Confession often, and to Holy Communion as frequently as my confessor allows.*
2. *I wish to sanctify Sundays and holy days in a special way.*
3. *My friends will be Jesus and Mary.*
4. *Death before sin!*

Over and over he repeated this last promise to the Immaculate Virgin, his beautiful white soul blazing with passion and love. His was a strong heart; he knew that the destructive and enticing lures of unchastity lay in wait for him; he knew he would be scorned and misunderstood for his devotion to purity; he knew the struggle to guard his innocence was perpetual and often overwhelming, and that alone it was impossible to win. But he knew also that with God and Our Lady fighting with him, he truly could win the victory and that he would rather die than yielding, offend his King and Queen in such a way. Yes, Dominic's heart was strong because his love was strong. His was a love that would accept death rather than inflict grief.

And so he repeated those words, essential to his charism, which would ring through the ages long after he had fulfilled them: "Death before sin..."

Dominic had always been an extraordinarily devout young Catholic. But this was when he placed his foot on the mountain of sainthood.

Four

"I've an idea, Massaglia."

"What's up?"

"Let's start a Sodality."

"What for?"

"Who for, you mean?" Dominic grinned. "Our Lady. In honor of her Immaculate Conception."

"Then you bet."

They approached a few other boys, Angelo, Cagliero, Bonetti, and Rua, and proposed the plan.

"What for?" Giovanni Bonetti cluelessly repeated.

"Our Lady."

"Yes, but what's the goal?"

Dominic answered with the straightest face. "To spread devotion to Our Lady."

They were sitting in a relatively quiet corner of the Oratory, eating their supper of stew and coarse bread.

"I haven't thought it all out yet," he added, looking round at their honest, interested faces. "All I really know is that I want to do something for her. Don Bosco approves of a Sodality. Maybe you fellows can help me come up with a way to go about it."

"We could start with receiving frequent Communion," Michael Rua suggested.

"That's always the start, isn't it," Angelo mused.

"You two sound just like Don Bosco." Cagliero stretched out his long legs and darted them a comical smile.

"That's good, then, it means we're right," Rua returned.

"If we're gonna make a Sodality for Our Lady," Bonetti interrupted with a calculating air, "we should ask Bongiovanni and Vaschetti to join."

"I vote Savio asks them," Massaglia declared.

"Same."

"How come?" Dominic wanted to know.

"Because everyone knows you're the Least Likely to Get Refused Award-Winner," Cagliero explained gravely. "In other words, everyone likes you. Oh, and a heads up: look out for Vaschetti. With all due respect to him, he's a monster."

"Then why are we asking him?" protested Angelo.

"We want him on our side," Bonetti grinned. "And he's got a good heart. It's just, well, you know. Disguised."

"Don't let him eat you, Savio," Massaglia advised.

"Gee, thanks."

Giuseppe Bongiovanni was easy enough to recruit. A sincere and devout youth, he was already good friends with Dominic and didn't hesitate a moment before accepting the invitation.

Next came the monster. Francesco Vaschetti was studying for a Latin test when Dominic came around, and he didn't want to be disturbed for a moment.

"Hey, Vaschetti!"

"Go away," snapped the reply from somewhere behind a book.

"I'll just be a minute."

"That's too long. Go away, before I swear at you in Latin."

Dominic felt annoyed. "You wouldn't swear in Italian, and everyone knows it. Now can't you be decent and listen to me for sixty seconds?"

"You've already wasted half of them." Vaschetti glared at him. "And no. *Amo, amas, amat —.*"

The saints have tempers, too. Dominic promptly lost his. Before he knew it, he had socked his antagonist right in the head, and Vaschetti was curled on the ground clutching his temples. Then both of them were groaning at the same time, Vaschetti because his head ached and Dominic because Saint Francis de Sales would have gone about the matter all too differently.

"Ughhhhh, Vaschetti, I'm so sorry!"

His moan was so full of dismay that Vaschetti laughed in spite of himself.

"Don't worry, just give me a hand, won't you?"

Still looking distressed, Dominic pulled Vaschetti to his feet. "Is it bad?"

"You bet! Just what I needed. Now I'll never forget what *amo, amas, amat* means. What were you asking?"

"Oh!" Dominic groaned again as if he'd been stabbed. "Just if you'd join a Sodality for Our Lady that I'm starting, but now I'm sure you'd rather join the Spartan army."

Vaschetti howled. "What a way to sell it! I like it, Savio! Put me on the list."

"All right, then," poor Dominic mumbled humbly. "Good luck on your test." He turned and made a beeline for the chapel.

The Sodality of the Immaculate Conception would not be officially established until many months later, but from the start it was a strong and close-knit force of the best boys in the Oratory. Their rules were practiced long before they were ever written. It was here that Dominic and his friends found spiritual support and loyal friendship in each other. And these grew as the members spent hours together organizing the Sodality, debating, praying, or simply having fun. Yet in no way were they a clique. That would have been detrimental to their goal. They were more of an underground army spread throughout the Oratory rescuing souls by befriending as many as possible.

Don Bosco knew this. He knew that the Sodality, like the Church itself, was missionary in identity. Therefore, he entrusted them with a secret task.

Many of his boys had led colorful and uninstructed lives before coming to the Oratory. These youngsters did not only need to learn the rules and schedule of the Oratory, they often needed to learn basic prayers as well. Not to mention many of them had little concern for the things of God which a good Oratory boy cherished.

It was these kids that Don Bosco quietly picked out and handed to the Sodalists. By a variety of tricks after their own boyish manner, they would try to turn their new companions around. Don Bosco found it very entertaining to watch them. And very satisfactory, as well.

It was with this in mind that he gazed at a ragged apprentice standing before him one chilly December morning.

"What's your name, son?"

"Giovanni Roda-Ambrè."

"Well, Giovanni, what can I do for you?"

"Would you let me stay at the Oratory, Father?" the boy begged.

Don Bosco smiled kindly and gestured to the only spare chair in the room. "Tell me about yourself. Who are your parents?"

"They're dead, Father."

"Ah." If he had been anyone else, Don Bosco would have been immune to the orphan's plight by now. But he could never. "I'm so sorry, my son," he said gently. "Where have you lived since then?"

"The streets. I'm an apprentice, but it hardly pays."

"I see. You haven't had a chance for an education?"

"No, Father."

"Well, Giovanni, I'd be happy to have you live here at the Oratory." He surveyed the elated boy for a moment, and an experienced guess told him what was needed. "I'm going to send for a boy who'll get you on your feet for your first few days. His name is Dominic Savio."

Roda immediately liked the clear-eyed youth who entered the room a few minutes later.

"Hello! Dominic Savio." Dominic stuck out his hand cordially and Roda shook it. An irrepressible grin was on the new boy's face.

"Why the big smile?" Dominic asked as they walked outside to tour the grounds.

"Just thinking," Roda answered, "I was kinda nervous to come, but not anymore."

"No? That's good. It's easy to feel at home here."

"Sure is. I felt that way the moment you came in the room."

"Gee, Roda, that's a nice thing to say! You'll love it here."

"Really? The fellas on the street said it's super holy and stuff."

Dominic tried not to laugh. "Do you think that's a bad thing?"

"I don't know," Roda shrugged. "I wouldn't really mind except..." He reddened uncomfortably.

"'Cept what?"

"Well, I don't know any prayers or anything."

"Oh, that's all?" Dominic put an arm around the newcomer's shoulder. "I've got you, then. We'll start with the Our Father. Repeat after me, ready?"

Dominic stayed by Roda's side the whole day, introducing him to the boys, explaining the rules and customs, and whenever there was a spare moment, teaching him his prayers.

That night, he lay awake staring at the cracks in the ceiling. He needed to plan his strategy, and now was the best time. Goodness, Angelo was snoring loudly. So he had Don Bosco's homilies, the Sodalists' prayers, and of course, heaven's grace, and he was dealing with a fellow who'd never been to the Sacraments and didn't know any prayers except half the Our Father. Not bad. Roda was certainly willing to learn about the Faith. That was a strong advantage.

Now for the battleplan. He'd attack as soon as Roda was up tomorrow morning and invite him to Mass. Then they'd have breakfast together and Dominic would find out if there were any ways he could help him feel more settled in. They'd chat a bit. That would put Roda at ease. Then he'd just have to look sharp for the best moment to fire his bullet and bring the subject around to God.

It wasn't a complicated formula, really. You simply showed you cared, and sooner or later they responded. Then you showed that *He* cared, and from there it all fell into place. His own efforts were clumsy enough, but God knew how to work through him.

So thinking, the little soldier dropped off to sleep.

———

Roda was more eager to accept the Faith than Dominic had realized. Much of this was because of Dominic's own contagious zeal. Characteristic of a true, humble Christian, the young warrior had forgotten to take himself into account when counting his troops.

Therefore, when Roda himself was the one to suggest they go over the Our Father the next morning, Dominic was pleasantly surprised.

"Of course! Let's see what you remember!"

"Oof, Savio, not much. You'll have to help me out. It's tricky-sounding."

"I know, I know. But let's see what you've got."

"Our Father, Who...um...does art in heaven! Uh...eh, I don't know what comes next." He dropped his head disconsolately. "I don't think I'll ever get to join in the prayers with the rest of you."

"Oh, none of that. You know, Roda, Saint Elizabeth of Hungary would begin the Our Father, and she'd only get that far — 'Our Father.' Then she'd get so caught up thinking about God being our Father that she wouldn't go on for another three hours. So you can think of her when you're stuck."

Roda let out a long whistle. "That's sure a long time to be thinking about two words! Guess she never got through a whole Rosary between two meals."

"Guess not."

"Well, anyway, what did I forget?"

"Hallowed be Thy Name."

"Our Father, Who art in heaven, hallowed...be Thy Name."

Over the next few days, Dominic hardly left his charge. Roda was more than grateful, yet in the presence of such a pure and good companion, he often felt filthy and troubled. His conscience was bothering him. He knew what he had to do to become happy and at ease like Dominic, but something within him fought vigorously against it. No, not yet...not yet...

Then one brisk afternoon, they played *bocce* together. The game was getting intense, and both of them had thrown all their energy into it. Dominic rolled his ball. Close. Again – closer. Then Roda went. He held his breath, aimed, leaned forward – the ball came up right next to Dominic's best. The two boys yelled in suspense. Roda aimed again. He was having the time of his life, and he liked Savio immensely.

Exactly what happened next he never knew, but somehow his ball went way out of whack, and he blasphemed roundly out of thoughtless habit.

No sooner did the words leave his mouth than Dominic let out an instinctive groan. His face was lined with a look of disappointment that Roda would never forget.

"Come on, my friend," he urged, coming up and putting a hand on the boy's shoulder. "Don't hurt Our Lord like that. He only speaks your name with love. Let's go to Don Bosco and clear that off your soul."

Confession – Roda went pale – no, that was supposed to be for later! But then, Savio was right. And what wouldn't he give to be happy like him? Surely it wasn't that great a price.

He went.

"Pray the Our Father as penance," Don Bosco told him, hiding a highly amused grin behind the grill. That young Savio worked fast.

Roda walked out on clouds. He'd never felt happier in his life. Why hadn't he done this earlier?

"Our Father, Who art in heaven...what came next? Oh, yes, hallowed be Thy Name."

Hallowed be Thy Name. Roda would never take that Name in vain again. And from then on, he went to Confession every week.

Professor Bonzanino, Dominic's teacher, caught on quickly. He had a number of rowdy and troublesome boys, but he soon figured out that none of them could keep up their roughness around Savio for long. So he merely sat them near Dominic and watched with grim satisfaction as they shed their wild ways within a few weeks. Every teacher should have a Savio, he thought blissfully. Just how the boy did it, he had no idea. There was no lofty lecturing or prim reprimanding, simply quiet example and a frank smile. But he did it, all right. He was sure as gold. Big, small, rich, poor, they succumbed to his holiness like flies in a web. And what's more, they enjoyed it. They'd only go to church kicking and screaming, but they flocked to Savio as if he were the governor waiting to bestow favors.

Professor Bonzanino wiped his spectacles and chuckled. He'd have a classroom of angels soon.

Had the good Professor known the full extent of Dominic's influence over his pupils, he would have been struck dumb. However, Dominic was silent over his victories. To him, it was enough that they were won. Thus, the following story is only known because the two offenders themselves told it to Don Bosco.

Caputto and Fabbri were two Oratory boys who attended Professor Bonzanino's classes with Dominic. They were tall, hefty lads, hardened by years of poverty but unbroken and headstrong in spirit. Personalities like theirs were destined to either bond tightly or clash severely. They clashed.

It happened when one of them insulted the family of the other, and the second returned the slight. The words grew harsher and louder until outraged, Caputto swore the only way to avenge his family honor was by a stone duel. Fabbri screamed back that he would be delighted to crush Caputto's skull with rocks, and they stormed off seething.

When Dominic got wind of what was happening, his teeth gritted resolutely.

"Not if I can help it," he muttered.

"Can you help it though, that's the question," his friend Bonetti debated. "Those guys are ten times bigger than you, and they look ready to kill."

Dominic politely ignored him.

Right away he set to work. He sought out the duelists separately and spoke to them. They refused to listen. He wrote them letters. No response. He pestered them, pleaded with them, threatened, reasoned, and stormed heaven with prayers. They remained unmoved.

Finally, at a loss, he threw himself at Our Lady's feet. "They're ready to kill each other! Please!" he entreated desperately. "Tell me what to do!"

It was then that an idea entered his head. Quickly, he looked up, and the battlelight entered his eyes.

———

"Fabbri! Wait up!"

"You again, Savio? Look, I'm happy to be friends with you, but stay out of this. I'm not gonna change my mind."

"Sure, I know. But since you're being so stubborn about it, at least agree to a condition."

"What's that?"

"I'll tell you when we get there."

Fabbri was startled. "Where? The duel?"

"You said it."

"Hey, look. You can't come. I tell you where and when it is, and you'll bring along Don Bosco to break it up."

"Not a bad idea. But I won't do that. I promise."

"What will you do then? I know you're gonna try to break it up somehow."

"I promise you I won't."

"Well fine then, as long as I can get my revenge on that Caputto —."
Fabbri swore so viciously that Dominic felt sick, but he bit his lip in silence.

Now for courage. Everything else was settled; Caputto had agreed in much the same way. Now he only needed courage, lots of it, please, Mamma...

It was very early in the morning when they set out, early so that no one else would discover them. The three boys headed for an empty field outside the town, Dominic often intervening to keep Caputto and Fabbri from flying at each other's throats on the way there.

When they reached the field, Dominic watched as the duelists gathered two heaps of sharp stones and tore off their jackets. His fingers were cold with sweat as he gripped a crucifix in his pocket. Courage, courage... The two boys glared at each other in hot hatred.

"We're ready. Give the signal, Savio," Caputto directed.

For purity, for Our Lady, for the love of God! — Dominic rushed into the space between them and held his crucifix high. "Go!" he cried.

"Get out!" Caputto ordered hoarsely. "You'll get killed!"

Taking a deep breath, Dominic shouted, "Here's the condition! Look at this crucifix and say, 'Christ was innocent and died forgiving his murderers, but I who am guilty want my revenge!' Then, throw your stone at me!"

The duelists stared blankly at the slight frame braced for pain.

"You get out, Savio!" Caputto repeated, now trembling.

In response, Dominic dashed to him and flung himself on his knees before the white-faced boy.

"Please, Caputto," he begged. "Throw your first stone at me. Let me have the first blow."

A cold chill went through Caputto's body. "No!" he gasped, covering his face. "I'd never hurt you, Savio! Never!"

Undeterred, his eyes blazing fire, Dominic ran to Fabbri.

"Then you throw!"

"No...no," Fabbri stammered in astonishment. "I won't hurt you either."

Dominic's face softened in earnest but gentle reproach. "And yet you would hurt Him by hurting each other." He lifted the crucifix again.

Caputto almost broke down.

"Will you forgive each other?" Dominic pleaded.

There was a long, tense moment of struggle. Then sounded a heavy *thud.* Caputto had dropped his stone. Fabbri bowed his head and dropped his. Seconds later their hands were clasped in forgiveness.

———

"Of all the stinking days to go to school, this is the absolute worst, and if old Bonzanino quotes Virgil at us one more time this week, I'm quitting!" Little, high-energy Giuseppe Reano began to swear violently and slam his books against the fence.

"Better be quiet, there," his friend warned. "Savio's coming."

The stream of profanity stopped like a shut faucet.

A warm spring wind was blowing from the south, tantalizing the group of Oratory boys with thoughts of summer as they walked to school. The city was packed shoulder to shoulder with carts, vendors, carriages, street urchins, soldiers, and officials, but somewhere beyond those dirty brick buildings there was nothing but peaceful streams running through lush green valleys, valleys just waiting, calling to be played in...

"I'm sick of school," Reano complained for the hundredth time. "School isn't meant for days like this. We're wasting our lives away sitting in that stuffy classroom."

"You're right," someone agreed. "Let's skip today."

"Don Bosco'd wallop us!" someone else protested.

"No he wouldn't. He'd just be sad and reason with us."

"Well, that's worse."

"Yeah, but he'll never know. Come on."

"Let's find a place outside town," Reano suddenly suggested, and that settled it. None of them could resist open fields on a spring day, especially when Virgil was the alternative.

None but Dominic. He hung back, trying his hardest not to think of swelling meadows and rickety fences like the ones back at home. How he'd love — but no, he couldn't —.

"Coming, Savio?" a one of the boys called.

"I'm not so sure."

The boys exchanged nervous glances. Not that Savio would tell on them, but Bonzanino would be suspicious if he showed up alone. Besides, they liked his company.

"C'mon, it'll be fun!" one of them urged. "There's nothing to do at school this time of year, anyway."

It was true. And the air in the classroom had been so thick yesterday it had been hard to breathe. Spring was just itching inside him. It couldn't be so bad to miss one day of school, after all. Only one day...

Taking a step forward, he opened his mouth to consent. But wait. One day. Did it matter how many days he skipped when every action had eternal consequences? Sinning the first time was just as wrong as sinning the millionth time, and often worse, because the first sin led to the millionth. No, he couldn't do it.

"Let's go to school, fellows," he said. "We can go outside town after."

It took some persuading, but in the end they all sat through a day of Virgil.

———

"Hey, Bonetti, what's up? Wanna make a visit to the chapel with me?"

Bonetti looked at Dominic wryly. "You know I wouldn't mind, but you stay in there *so* long."

Dominic grinned. "You think I'd tackle you if you tried to leave before me? Come on."

Bonetti shook his head in good-natured helplessness and went.

"Ever thought about how amazing it must be to be a priest?" Dominic asked him as they walked. "To be the one who brings Our Lord physically into the world! What a holy vocation!"

Suddenly, Bonetti felt a strange jump in his heart. A priest... He gave his friend a sidelong glance. He had known priests all his life, yet this had never occurred to him before. A priest...

"Hey, Ratazzi!" Dominic called. "Wanna make a visit?"

"You're nuts!" Bonetti hissed. "He'd go to jail before going to church!"

"Absolutely not!" Ratazzi yelled rudely. "Go by yourself with your measly friend if you want!"

Bonetti started forward hotly but Dominic caught his wrist. Meanwhile, one of Ratazzi's companions fetched the scoundrel a clout on the head.

"Don't you talk to Savio like that!" he flashed. "Wait up, Savio, *I'll* come with you!"

"See," Dominic told Bonetti, "it's always worth the effort."

Dominic's love for the Holy Eucharist was profound, as it is in every soul who truly recognizes the consecrated Host as God. He had always cherished the Eucharist. From the days of his early childhood when he would kneel outside in all kinds of weather until the church doors were unlocked, to the time when he was permitted to receive his First Holy Communion five years before the other children his age, to the present when he dragged his schoolmates with him to pray in the chapel, Dominic had shown an abiding and fervent devotion to his Jesus in the Tabernacle.

In those days the dark heresy of Jansenism prevented many people from receiving the Eucharist frequently. Most Catholics would go to Mass often yet only receive Communion once or twice a year. Thus, before coming to the Oratory, Dominic had only received the Eucharist once a month. "You are not worthy!" warned the Jansenists, but Don Bosco replied that the Mercy of God is greater than our unworthiness. One of his most consistent themes was the frequent reception of Holy Communion. That and frequent Confession. Again and again he preached on these, and soon Dominic was receiving Communion every two weeks. Then every week. Then multiple times a week. He went to Confession every week. But for him this still was not enough. He loved his Lord and wanted to be united to Him as fully as possible, so he visited Him often in the Oratory chapel and brought his classmates along whenever he could.

And still he wanted more.

His eyes glued adoringly upon the white Host in the monstrance, Dominic entreated silently, "Every day, Jesus! Let me receive You in Communion every day!"

There is no greater gift in this world.

———————

It was a rainy morning in April. A morning Dominic would never forget.

It started out like any other. He woke up to the sound of two fellows arguing over whose shoe was whose and shouted with laughter with the rest of the dorm when it was discovered that the shoes were three sizes apart. Then he rolled out of bed onto his knees to offer the day to God, washed and dressed, and went to Mass. Massaglia slipped in beside him, and soon the Mass began.

Outside, the rain was pouring down in sheets, and Dominic had to struggle against its lulling droning to keep himself awake. *It's God!* he told himself fiercely. *I can't stay awake for God?*

Then Don Bosco began to preach. And suddenly he was no longer tired. It was as if he were lifted out of the world onto a different plane, where only one thing mattered, and that one thing was so clear.

"Saint Francis Xavier was once a boy your age, with thoughts of sports and fun. Saint Francis of Assisi was once twelve and thirteen and fourteen years old, craving fame, battle, and glory. Saint Paul was once a young student like you. They were young and human, with faults, virtues, dreams, and passions. And they became saints. *Why not you?* It is not just your calling to become a saint, but your duty. This is what you were created for. Sainthood is not just for the saints who have already been canonized. No, my boys, it's for every single one of you, too. *Every single one* of you. You think it's hard – you think it's impossible because so few have done it compared to how many should. But I'll tell you something. The saints found it just as hard as you do. And they did it. How? Because it was so hard that they realized they could never do it alone. They saw how unworthy and helpless they were, so they turned to the only One Who could help them. God. God gave them their holiness, and He will give *you* your holiness, too, if you turn to Him sincerely. Not only that, my sons, but God will turn sainthood from something impossible to something easily attainable, if you only give Him your will. If only you try, my boys! He wants your sainthood more than you *can* want it. Do you really think He would stand by and watch you strive for it without flying to help you? No! All He wants is your true effort and your will. He will make you saints, as He made Francis Xavier a saint, as He made Francis of Assisi a saint..."

So He will make Dominic Savio a saint. The boy's eyes were flaming intensely, his fists clenched whitely, his frame trembling with passion. He *must* become a saint – nothing else was necessary. He would do everything he could, and it would never be enough, but God would help him. God would bring about the victory as He had for Francis Xavier, Aloysius Gonzaga, Teresa of Avila, Alphonsus Liguori, Joan d'Arc – so He would do it for Dominic Savio. They had once been like him, young, afraid of contempt, overwhelmed by the sheer vastness of true holiness; but someday he, Dominic Savio, would be like them – a saint. Someday, he would stand in their number. And until his dying breath, nothing else would be his goal.

Five

The days passed, and Dominic's yearning for sainthood became so painfully ardent that it seemed to consume him. He could scarcely think of anything else. He spent hours in the chapel, and for the first time since he had come to the Oratory, he became so quiet and withdrawn that his companions wondered if there was something wrong with him. This was not the sunny, easy-going Savio they were used to.

Little did they know he was burning up inside.

Don Bosco noticed the change as well and began to worry.

"Dominic," he summoned to him one day. "Is something wrong? You've been very quiet lately."

"No, Father. It's something good!"

"Something good?"

A fierce light blazed into the youth's eyes, and he took a deep breath, then opened his soul to the listening priest.

"Remember that homily you gave about sainthood? Well, ever since then, my longing to become a saint has become so strong I often feel I can't bear it, but it just keeps getting stronger! I'm glad of it, but I don't know what to do, Father! I'm not making enough progress. I'm not doing enough, and I feel like I'll never be able to do enough, but I want it so badly, and...I don't know how to explain it, but I feel rushed. I need to become a saint *quickly.* And if I don't become one, I'm a total failure."

The look in his face was so intense that Don Bosco placed his hands on the boy's shoulders and said, "It's wonderful that you want to become a saint, but first, Dominic, you have to calm yourself. If you aren't calm, how will you be able to hear the voice of God? You must be calm and cheerful at all times."

"You mean I can become a saint by being happy?" Dominic asked dubiously.

Don Bosco grinned. "Come, now, you really think the saints were as solemn-faced as people make out? They were the happiest people on earth!"

"Why?"

"Because God was so close to them."

"I guess that makes sense. But that's not enough, I'm sure."

"You're right. You must also do your duties well and be exact in your practices of holiness."

"That's it?! But the saints went around nursing the sick and converting pagans and building churches and monasteries! How can I become a saint by studying my Latin?"

"Because that's your duty. That's what God wants of you right now. He wanted those things of other people, but you're your own case."

"I feel like a pretty lousy case, then."

"Nonsense. You can do a lot of good right where you are. I'll give you one more piece of advice, and that's to help your companions. One of the first things to do in becoming a saint is to help others become saints. Saint Patrick had the Irish, Saint Francis Xavier had the Indians, Saint Boniface had the Germans, and you —." He brought Dominic to the window and pointed to a shouting, running throng of boys. "You have the Oratory boys. Now go have fun with them, and bring them to Our Lord. Go set them on fire."

Immersed in thought, Dominic looked from the crowd of boys to Don Bosco. A slow little smile dawned on his face. Then he ran from the room, straight into the heart of his mission.

Watching him, Don Bosco smiled. Mamma Margaret was right – there was something remarkable about that young fellow. He thought about Roda, about Caputto and Fabbri, about the boys on the nearby streets who would drop their dirty language like a hot iron the moment they saw him coming, about so many others who had changed their ways just by being around him. In Don Bosco's mind, there was no question.

Sitting down at his desk, he opened a drawer and drew out a stack of papers written in his own hand. As he leafed through them, story after edifying story rose before his mind, with young Savio playing the lead role in each of them. No, there was no doubt. And someday these papers would be needed.

Don Bosco turned to the first page and dipped his pen in ink. At the top of the paper he scrawled in large, even letters: *The Life of Dominic Savio.* Then he flipped to the first empty sheet and began to write.

———————

Dominic, meanwhile, had run himself into trouble. He had started talking about a saint, and while most of the boys listened willingly, a few of them were less than interested.

"Would you just drop it, Savio?" the old troublemaker Ratazzi snapped. "Why do you care so much?"

Dominic wheeled on him belligerently. "Because Jesus cared enough to die, that's why! And because as friends we oughta be helping each other out!"

Ratazzi was cowed into silence.

Later that day, Dominic hunted down Massaglia and told him what Don Bosco had advised.

"I've decided to become a saint," he said. "Wanna do it with me?"

Massaglia choked. "Easier said than done, but of course."

"All right, then. See, this is the best way to be friends, because we'll see each other in heaven, too."

"That's true," the boy answered grimly. "But the hard part is getting there."

"Come on, Massaglia, weren't you listening to Don Bosco the other day? It's not that hard. All you need to do is try your best, and God's Mercy will fill whatever's lacking."

"Yeah, but trying your best is hard work. I'll do it, though," Massaglia promised, laughing as Dominic pretended to punch him. "Lent is coming up, you know."

"I know. What are you going to do for it?"

"I want to fast for certain meals. Have you read the book Don Bosco wrote about his friend in seminary?"

"*The Life of Comollo*? Yes."

"Well, it talks a lot about penance, you know, and how penance is necessary for real holiness because it keeps you fervent."

"And for purity," Dominic added.

"Yeah. *The Imitation of Christ*, too, talks about penance on pretty much every page."

"So, I guess we'll be doing extra penances this Lent!"

"Right! What are you thinking of doing?"

"I don't know, eating fish on Fridays? No, just kidding. I'm going to try to find a hairshirt."

"Just where on earth are you gonna get one of those?" Massaglia demanded. "I thought they were extinct!"

"I'm not sure. Maybe I'll ask Don Bosco."

If Dominic wanted a hairshirt, Don Bosco was the very last person he should have gone to. The priest was horrified.

"A *hairshirt?!!* You can be certain you won't get one of those, not while I'm alive!"

"But Father, I've got to do *something* for Lent!"

"Well, there are a good deal of other somethings you can do. Now get out, and don't let me hear that word from you again!"

There went the hairshirt, Dominic thought ruefully.

The rain had caked Turin in mud. All the streets in the city were thick with the filth. Carefully, Dominic picked his way through, racking his brain for good penances.

"You could cut holes in the toes of your socks," Angelo suggested. "That's the worst feeling ever."

"Yeah, but Mamma Margaret would darn them the next day."

"You're right. Well —."

Just then they heard the bells of an altar boy, and from around the corner came a priest carrying the Blessed Sacrament. Down on his knees went Dominic, right into the mud.

I love You, dearest Jesus! Thank You for coming to us in this Sacrament — that was it! He would ask to receive daily Communion! His face glowed.

"Gee, Dominic," Angelo wrinkled his nose once the priest was gone from sight. "You didn't need to kneel in the mud! Just look at your trousers! God wouldn't want you to get them all dirty like that."

"No?" Dominic retorted in thorough disagreement. "Trousers as well as knees belong to God and therefore should be used in His honor." His face softened a little. "It's God, Angelo. We should be willing to not just throw ourselves into mud but even into a fiery furnace when we enter His Presence. Then our love would be like His, burning and pure."

Angelo squirmed and trusted himself to luck that the next time the Blessed Sacrament passed him in the street, the ground would be a bit drier.

———

Dominic took his mission of helping the Oratory boys extremely seriously. The troublemakers were his chief target. He went at them with a passion, and they never knew what had hit them until they were kneeling in the confessional wondering how they had gotten there. The sick and the excluded, too, were his special concern, as well as any new kids. As always, his thoughtful compassion won him the confidence of many a lad. The faces of forgotten cripples shone with delight when they saw him approaching — Savio, the popular, happy fellow whom everyone wanted to be around, was coming to them. The new boys warmed to his smile when they looked on a sea of unfamiliar faces and found him coming forward to greet them. The invalids cheered weakly when he entered the sickroom to talk with them and nurse them. He was just another thirteen-year-old boy, yet he managed to touch and transform so many lives by quietly doing his duty, looking out for the outcasts, and above all, giving everything to Jesus through Mary.

On a cool Sunday afternoon, a knot of his friends watched as he led a boy towards the chapel.

"If he gets that kid to Confession, he's a saint," Bongiovanni declared flatly.

"A saint wouldn't have punched me in the head," Vaschetti contradicted.

"Anyone would punch you in the head," Cagliero returned.

"Well, that's a good point," Vaschetti agreed. "At any rate, Savio can get anyone to do what he wants. You know that when he lugs rough kids like that one off to Confession, because Confession's the last place most people want to go."

"Not Savio," Bonetti said. "He's in there himself every week."

"How? What does he even confess?"

"Beats me."

"Bless me, Father, for I have sinned. I forgot to button the top button of my shirt."

"Pretty much. Though I'm sure *he* finds enough. Has anyone else noticed he's receiving Communion every day now?"

"You're an altar rail observer, I see. I didn't notice. Not surprised, though. He basically lives on the Sacraments."

"Know what he told me?" Cagliero grinned. "I asked him once, 'Hey, Savio, how come you're always so happy?' and he said, 'It's pretty simple. If anything's bothering my conscience, I go to Confession, and it goes away. If I need anything, I go to Communion, and I get it! What more could a fellow ask?' So I went off and thought about it, and you know, it makes a lot of sense. Sufferings and annoyances don't really bother him because he just offers them up to God. Therefore, only a bad conscience could upset him. And God is All, so he really does get everything in Communion. Besides, God does answer every prayer in one way or another. I think I'll try it myself. It seems to work for him."

"I got it!" Bongiovanni slammed his knee. "The Sacraments are what make him so holy! He told me to visit the Blessed Sacrament a lot if I want a lot of graces. He sure does. I'll bet that's his secret."

"Then how come so many people receive the Sacraments all the time but don't seem changed by them?" Bonetti questioned.

Angelo had been listening but hadn't said anything. Now he looked up. "Dominic takes them seriously," he answered.

Dominic had a big problem. Don Bosco wouldn't let him fast. He had been all ready to fast on bread and water every Saturday in honor of Our Lady, and then Don Bosco had popped that plan like a pin going into a balloon. Well, he'd just have to join Massaglia in some less extreme fasting. He could start by skipping the next meal.

That plan lasted a full week. Then Don Bosco found out.

"Mamma Margaret tells me you haven't been eating as much," he brought up, trying to sound stern.

Dominic reddened.

"Just for Lent," he protested feebly.

"Well, no more of that." When Don Bosco realized how crestfallen his young charge was, his tone relaxed. After all, how could one truly be upset over such a beautiful thing? "Now, Dominic, you have to take care of your health. You're not very strong as it is."

"Can I at least go without breakfast?"

"Good heavens!" Don Bosco threw his hands into the air. "No, Dominic, I want you eating three square meals a day, and that's that!"

So now Dominic's problem was even bigger. How could he become a saint without fasting? All the saints had done it, as far as he knew — some hadn't eaten at all, except for the Eucharist, and here he had to eat three meals a day? He had to do penance to keep himself pure and free from spiritual laziness, and besides, he wanted to do it as a love offering to Jesus and Mary.

Suddenly he had an idea. He went outside and gathered up some stones and chips of wood. Finding a thorn bush, he broke off a few branches and brought those along, too. It would remind him of the Crown of Thorns. A few nut shells were scattered on the ground, and he scooped them up and added them to the collection. Then he went to his dorm, dumped them all on his bed, spread them out evenly, and covered them with the blanket. Plan E was under way.

That night was agony. Every way he turned, he felt himself poked and cut. He hardly slept.

"For you, Mamma!" he prayed, suffering in silence. "For purity!"

He knew it was worth keeping himself pure. He knew Christ had suffered infinitely more. Still, he couldn't help thinking wryly to himself a few times that he wouldn't be entirely disappointed if Don Bosco put an end to it.

———————

The Oratory boys crowded around Don Bosco's chair one evening as they did every night before going to bed. He was telling them about the meaning of names, while they sat sprawled out on the floor and looked up attentively at his loving countenance.

"Giovanni — there's a bunch of us Giovannis in here, eh? Cagliero, Massaglia, Roda, Bonetti... Your name means 'God is gracious.' Giuseppe? Where are my Giuseppes? Ah, yes, your name means 'God will add.' See, these are good names and you'd better live up to them. My Luigis?"

On he went through the names. Listening carefully, Dominic mused on how beautiful the meanings were. How splendid to be called 'God is gracious'! One's whole life should then be a special testament to the Mercy of God. What should his whole life point to, he wondered? He raised his hand.

"What does 'Dominic' mean, Father?"

"Ah! Dominic." A tender smile lighted Don Bosco's face. How

appropriate this name for its owner! "Dominic means 'of the Lord,'" he answered.

Dominic's whole visage radiated with joy. Of the Lord! How forcefully everything pointed him toward the one mission of his life — sainthood!

"See!" he cried elatedly. "Even my name tells me I belong to God! Therefore I *have* to become a saint!"

The information seemed to electrify him. He belonged to God; thus, he had to become as perfect as possible. He poured his heart into making his soul as pure as he could; he called on Mary, the saints, and his Guardian Angel to fill him with virtue; he prayed and made sacrifices and leapt to the aid of others. "Let no occasion for doing good to souls or of offering some little act of reparation to God be missed," was his driving motto. Let no chance go unseized.

Yet still he slipped, and he knew it. He also knew there were times he slipped without knowing it. He needed a monitor, someone who would tell him whenever he fell short of perfection. Someone who knew his tendencies and habits, who was with him throughout the day, who shared his zeal for holiness. Who else but Giovanni Massaglia? (Don Bosco was already monitoring him.) Yes, Massaglia was the one.

When he asked, Massaglia stared at him. "Correct...what?" he stammered.

"Whatever you see wrong in me. You know, lots of times we have faults we don't even notice, like making faces when people say things — that kind of thing. Or if there's any good I should add, tell me. Please?"

"I mean, I will if I see anything, but really, Savio, that just won't happen. You should be the one doing this for me."

Dominic's answer was point blank. "Look, let's forget the compliments and help make each other saints. Deal?"

Massaglia looked at him and broke into a grin. "Deal."

May was always a special month for Dominic, for no other reason than that it was Mary's month. He had always made it a point to offer up some kind of sacrifice in her honor each day, but now he stepped this up. He roused his Sodality friends to pray to her together daily and talked about her whenever he found the chance. Scores of boys celebrated the month with special devotion because of him. But still it wasn't enough.

Bonetti came up with the idea of erecting an altar dedicated to Our Lady in their dorm. The boys agreed eagerly. They contributed money to buy candles, flowers, cloth, a statue – anything and everything they could possibly need.

Dominic, however, didn't have a cent in his pocket. He and a few other boys, also broke, watched dismally as the collection grew and they could add nothing to it.

Then one day an idea struck him like a thunderbolt. Smiling wildly, he rushed to his other penniless friends and gathered them up in a corner of the Oratory field.

"Listen, I have a book that some of the fellows here might like. I'm going to sell it –."

"You do need a new shirt," one of them agreed.

"No!" Dominic laughed, so contagiously that the whole group smiled with him. "I'm going to put the money in the altar fund!"

A shout went up of infected jubilation.

"You got *brains*, Savio! I'm doing it with you!"

The boys tore through the Oratory, Dominic at their head. They burst into their dorm and wreaked havoc tossing any of their potentially desirable possessions into a pile. They set up a lottery and yelled at their friends to buy tickets. Before long, they had a wonderful sum of money in their hands and were poorer than ever. But now they had a part in decorating their Lady's altar.

The things they bought for her were lovely, and the penniless boys glowed more than anyone else when they saw them. Dominic glowed more than any of the penniless boys. The altar was to be adorned after Compline one night, and for hours, Dominic looked forward to it in delight. But he was starting to feel sick, and woe to him, Don Bosco noticed it. He was to go to bed right after Compline.

When Dominic heard this, it was hard to keep back the groan of disappointment. He heard his friends talking eagerly about decorating the altar and bit his lip in bitter silence. Why did it have to be this way? But Mary had obeyed, and Jesus had obeyed, even when faced with Calvary.

Compline ended, the boys of his dorm ran to adorn Mary's altar with flowers and candles, and Dominic went to bed. Above all, obedience was necessary.

———————

Dominic's love for Our Lady didn't stop with sacrifices, building the altar, or even obedience. It carried into every moment of his life. More than anything, it bastioned his effort for purity. Mary had been entirely immaculate; how fitting then, to serve her by remaining pure!

It was such thoughts that filled his mind one afternoon as he and his friends were walking through Turin. The city was a pitfall even for the holiest, and Dominic was not unaware. He would have had to be blind not to know that. The sights that filled the town were jarringly unchaste.

Immaculate Mother, protect me. There was a sin of the eyes, and he was not about to commit it. Once an image entered your head, chances were it might never leave. It would torture you, you would become calloused to it, then you would allow yourself to look at another like it for a fraction of a second longer than you had the first. That fraction of a second was fatal, because it always grew. Bit by bit, your mind would become filthier and wouldn't be capable of contemplating God in all His purity as it once had. If he wanted to remain pure, he knew, he must persevere in his innocence.

So he kept his eyes down. His eyes were kept fixed on the ground and his mind on the heavens. In tender love, he contemplated Our Lady in all her glorious innocence and marveled at how stunningly gorgeous she must be because of it.

Meanwhile, his head began to ache. The urge to look up – just once, just for a moment, just to make sure it wasn't that bad – pounded against his temples and screamed at him with almost overwhelming fury. If he had not already been in the habit of resisting his senses, he would have given way immediately. But no, he would not look up; Sweet Mary, save him! Look to her instead...

Despair began to assail him. How could he keep doing this multiple times a day, causing himself a fierce headache every time he merely walked through the streets? Day after day, week after week, month after month, stretching to who knew how long – someday he would have to give in, so why not now? But Dominic was firm. He kept his eyes on the ground. If he won this battle, he would be more likely to win the next.

Still, the struggle stormed inside him. Will-power against hot impulse, built-up resolve against burning curiosity, grace against shrieking evil. Just once, just for one moment –.

"Did you see that?" one of the boys cried.

The rest of them assented in excitement. Only Dominic said nothing.

"Did you see that, Savio?" they asked eagerly.

"I must have missed it," he answered with quiet modesty.

Don't look – but surely it wouldn't be bad – *don't look!*

"Come on, Savio," someone snubbed him. "Whad'ya got eyes for, anyway?"

Dominic grappled with all the powers of his soul against the deafening screams of temptation. *Mary!* his heart wept out, and all of a sudden he saw her, radiant with the beauty of purity. All the storms of agony were stilled, and he gazed back at her with a celestial smile of tranquility.

To his clueless companions he gave the poignant reply: "I have eyes to gaze at the Mother of God when I get to heaven."

———

Don Bosco looked through a stack of papers. Bonetti was doing well, getting good grades; Ratazzi...he passed a hand through his hair and sighed. The boy seemed hopeless. Terrible grades and making all kinds of trouble in class, too. Savio — now here was a breath of fresh air. Professor Bonzanino had passed him for two years in one because the lad had already studied Latin in Mondonio under Father Cugliero. The report was followed with glowing praise. Dominic wasn't naturally brilliant, but he worked so hard that he was one of the top in the class. Don Bosco liked that kind. Now for the next class. Here was Massaglia. He would be ready to enter seminary at the end of the summer —.

There was a mild uproar from one of the dorms. As Don Bosco glanced up, his mother flew through the door.

"You have to put an end to this, Giovanni, or he'll kill himself by accident! Just look what I found!"

He looked at the rocks and thorns in Mamma Margaret's hands. "Who? Put an end to what?"

"Dominic Savio, and who else? I went to wash the sheets, and these were in his bed!"

Don Bosco almost hit the ceiling. "Where is that impossible boy?" he roared.

A few minutes later, the impossible boy was standing before him very meekly.

"But I need to become a saint, Father," he argued humbly.

Don Bosco forced himself to remain composed, but inside he wanted to yell at the boy for not taking care of himself and at the same time break down because his devotion was so moving.

"All things in moderation, except for love, but *especially* in penance, and especially for you," he commanded. "It's not healthy for a growing boy your age to be undertaking such drastic penances, especially when you're already not as strong as you should be." He scanned the lad's pale face and added drily, "I think I know what's been contributing to that lately. If you must do penances, son, they'll have to be small ones."

"Like what?" Dominic asked forlornly.

"Hold your tongue when you're angry, guard your eyes from impure sights, obey cheerfully, and so on."

"But I already do that. I want to do more."

It was true, Don Bosco thought. Such things were habit for Dominic.

"Mortify yourself in the small comforts, then. The very small comforts, mind you. For example, if you like to keep your hands in your pockets, take them out. That's what I mean by small." He grinned. "I call them 'pious dodges.'"

The old undisturbed happiness returned to Dominic's face. "All right, Father, I'll do that! Thank you!" He headed for the door.

"I said small, Dominic!" the priest called after him. "Don't forget it!"

"Yes, Father!"

Don Bosco looked after him sharply for a moment, then went back to his stack of papers.

———————

"Ugh, this stew is nasty!" Tomatis complained.

Dominic just grinned. "Don't thank Mamma Margaret that way." Inside he was elated because he had something to offer up. He glanced around and caught sight of what he was looking for, a boy eating alone in a corner. "C'mon, Tomatis, let's make a friend."

Giuseppe Momo, a shy, reserved fellow whom the others easily forgot about, lit up when the well-loved Dominic sat next to him.

"What's up, Momo?"

"Not much. How 'bout you?"

"Just enjoying my dinner." Dominic thrust a mischievous wink at the disgusted Tomatis. "Wanna hear what I did to Cagliero today?"

Dominic was a conversation king. He never interrupted anyone who was speaking, but if uncomfortable silence or idle complaining entered the scene, he knew just what to say to get rid of it. Lots of times he sensed when it was coming and intercepted it with some story or remark that sent the boys doubling over with laughter. They loved when he was around.

Momo hung onto his words in delight. Dominic noticed it and began to thrust in gentle hints about going to the Sacraments. Bit by bit, he turned the conversation around until he and Tomatis were telling funny stories that had happened to them in Confession. Momo just sat and listened. Just as the meal was about to end, Dominic shot his bullet.

"Say, since we're talking about it, why don't you come to Confession with me on Saturday?"

Silence dropped.

"Ehhhh," Tomatis wriggled in his seat, until Dominic smiled at him hopefully. Then he gave up. "Fine, I'll go."

Dominic turned to Momo, who shrugged carelessly and replied, "Suits me."

Tomatis left a few moments later. Before Dominic could think of anything to say to Momo, the latter leaned forward earnestly and said in a low voice, "Tell me, Savio, what makes you so on fire with love? I want to be good, but I give up so easily. Meantime, you just get better."

"It's Our Lady," Dominic told him readily, breaking into a happy glow at the mention of her name. "She's so eager to make us saints, Momo. If you can just tap that source, she'll fill you with grace."

"How do I do that?"

"Just ask her. But be sincere. The more sincere you are, the more graces she'll give you."

"I'll try it," the boy resolved.

"Do that. And if you'd like, you should join our Sodality. We talk about her all the time."

Momo's face shone. All his reserve had vanished. "I'd love to!" he cried, and another member was added to Mary's little military unit.

At that point supper had just ended, and the two lined up to wash their utensils. Dominic was astonished at how easily the boy suddenly opened up to him, asking all kinds of questions and devouring his answers. They chatted until it was time for Don Bosco's evening talk, then sat with the rest before the priest's chair. Don Bosco's vigorous hushing drew silence over the room.

"I have an announcement that you'll all like," Don Bosco said. "June twenty-fourth is the feast of my patron Saint John the Baptist. Therefore, I'd like to give each of you a little gift —." They roared in appreciation until he managed to shush them again. "Leave a piece of paper on my desk saying what you'd like, and I'll do my best to get it for you. Sound good?" They howled and cheered again, and he grinned, then yelled over them to begin his talk.

It was on sainthood again. Dominic focused all his attention on Don Bosco as if he were trying to memorize each sentence verbatim. Sainthood. How sweet the word was, how daunting, how alluring! It hung over him like a golden cloud of mystery, yet when he approached it, it was so strikingly simple and clear. Love. Love was all that was needed. True, uncalculating love — love that issued straight from the Heart of the Trinity and sped right back into It — love that would suffer torture and death for one's enemies — love that would accept and spread the Truth unflinchingly — love that would choose death before sin. It was so simple and clear, so sweet yet painfully demanding. So beautiful, so vital, and how he *thirsted* for it with insatiable longing!

Momo noticed with a start that his friend was literally trembling with passion and looked up anxiously at Don Bosco. The priest had stopped speaking. Now he was making his way to Dominic while the boys cleared a way for him.

"Come, my son."

The two saints left the room.

Alone together, Don Bosco laid a soothing hand on Dominic's shoulder and asked gently, "Are you all right?"

"Yes." The boy breathed a deep, shaky sigh. "I want it so much, Father! So much!"

"I know. God is good. He will make you a saint."

"I trust in Him."

The next morning, Don Bosco found a folded slip of paper on his desk. Ah, this would be a gift request. He opened it and read. Then he put it down heavily as the tears crept to his eyes.

"Make me perfect," it read.

Signed, Dominic Savio.

Six

Massaglia opened the church door and peered in. The stillness inside was almost a sound in itself. He waited a moment as his eyes adjusted to the dim lighting, then gazed adoringly upon the Tabernacle. Dear God! He was to become a priest! In a few short months he would enter the seminary – the thought! The precious, heart-throbbing, unthinkable thought! That by his own words, like Mary, he would someday call the Son of God into the world; that with his hands, like Christ, he would give that Body to hungering souls! How could any man have dared imagine such a privilege had it not been that the Mercy of God initiated it! Stunned, crushed with gratitude, Massaglia knelt down while his heart pounded with love. Like Christ, the Source of Grace, like Mary, the Mediatrix of Grace, he would stand between God and man, giving his whole life in order to bring God to man and man to God. What a sacred and noble duty was the priest's, yet how terrible with glory! No man could ever be worthy of it, yet here was Massaglia, his heart empty so God could fill it with the only worthiness in the universe – His Divine own...

With a little shiver, Massaglia returned to earth and withdrew his eyes from the Tabernacle. He threw a glance around the church. There he was.

The fellow who'd sent him from a trot to a hard sprint along the road to heaven. God bless him and make more like him!

Cautiously, he walked to Dominic's pew and leaned forward to catch a glimpse of his face. His eyes were closed and his lips slightly open. His whole countenance breathed such an aura of angelic and radiant peace that Massaglia paused, struck with reverent awe. He had no right, but he had been ordered.

Hesitantly, he touched Dominic's shoulder and softly whispered his name. The boy's lids opened slowly, and he glanced around confused; then his brows cleared and he sighed.

"I'm sorry," he apologized humbly. "I got distracted again." His tone was one of regret.

Massaglia felt a chill running down his spine. It had happened three times now in the past two weeks. Dominic would go to Communion and forget to come back. It reminded one of Saint Catherine of Siena, who would be so united with her Eucharistic Love that she would not even feel the pin pricks of curious onlookers... Massaglia shook himself.

"We're eating breakfast now," he said in a low voice. "And we're having our last Sodality meeting, remember, before the schoolyear ends."

"Oh, right."

Dominic seemed embarrassed, and as they left, Massaglia wisely spoke not a word about it. Still, his mind raced. It was hard to imagine that the glowing saint he had seen inside the church was the same cheerful, popular friend he knew so well. Yet was it so hard? Savio was Savio. As much as Massaglia felt he ought to be shaken in his presence, he couldn't help but feel at ease. He thrust a glance at his friend. Sainthood was such a strange thing.

"What's for breakfast?" Dominic asked, and suddenly Massaglia was nearly choking with laughter.

"What's so funny?"

"Nothing." Nothing except that the saints ate, too, and that was such a colossal relief. "Mind if I ask a question?"

"'Course not."

"You once asked me how to pay attention all through Mass. Now I'm asking you, how do you receive Communion so devoutly?"

"It's the same question, really, and the same answer, too." Dominic gazed into the distance and smiled. "It's God." They were silent for a while, then he added, "The more we believe that the Host we receive is really God, the more it drives away any other thoughts."

"And I guess that makes our preparation and thanksgiving more fervent, too."

"Sure does."

"Can I ask how you prepare yourself?"

"Well," Dominic's brow clouded a little. "It's impossible to ever be worthy of Him, you know, but I use all the time I've got. I divide the day in two. My preparation begins at three o'clock in the afternoon the day before (that gives me about eight waking hours) and then my thanksgiving ends at three (also eight hours) so I can begin preparing for my next Communion."

"So strategic you are," Massaglia laughed.

"Why, thank you!" Dominic brushed off the compliment and joined in the other's laughter.

"I've been looking for ways to receive Him more devoutly," Massaglia continued, more seriously, "because you're right. He is God, and He deserves all we've got. But I just know I'm not doing enough."

"We can never do enough, Massaglia," Dominic answered softly. "He's the Creator and we're the creatures. But here, look at this if you'd like. I find that offering each day's Communion for a specific intention makes me receive Him more fervently."

He drew a wrinkled piece of paper from his pocket, and Massaglia read it:

Sunday: In honor of the Blessed Trinity.

Monday: For my spiritual and material benefactors.

Tuesday: In honor of my patron saint, Saint Dominic, and of my Guardian Angel.

Wednesday: In honor of Our Lady's Seven Sorrows, for the conversion of sinners.

Thursday: For the souls in Purgatory.

Friday: In honor of the Sacred Passion of Christ.

Saturday: In honor of Our Lady, for her protection in life and death.

"Strategic again," said Massaglia. "Mind if I copy it?"

"Not at all. 'Cept don't forget that Saint Dominic isn't your patron saint."

"You buffoon!" Massaglia nudged him roughly then turned on him with a wide smile. "I've got news."

"Tell me!"

"I'm entering the seminary this fall."

"You tyrant, why didn't you tell me before?!" Dominic nearly knocked him over in a bear hug. "Oh, Massaglia, that's wonderful!" His eyes shone every bit as much as his friend's. "It's settled, then?"

"Yes. Don Bosco told me after Mass."

"I can hardly believe it! Oh, Massaglia! I've never felt so jealous in my life, except when my sister Raimonda got the biggest piece of my birthday cake when I turned five, but I'm over that now. Oh, I'm so happy for you!"

Up ahead, Don Bosco smiled to himself as he saw the two coming to breakfast. What a good, wholesome pair!

"Good morning, boys!" he called out. "Hungry?"

"Morning, Don Bosco! You bet!"

"Almost done the year, eh?" he said, as Mamma Margaret scooped the last of the porridge into their bowls. "Are you all ready to go home for the summer?"

"Well..." Massaglia hesitated awkwardly. The two boys glanced at each other. "We'd actually rather stay here, if that's all right."

"Why's that?" Don Bosco was surprised.

They looked at each other again, grinning.

"What's that smile for, now?" the priest inquired in amusement.

"Well, Father," Dominic explained, "we're much safer here. As much as we'd love to see our families – well, you know, a little bird is safer in a cage because the hawks can't get it. Here at the Oratory we have a schedule and everything we need to grow in holiness, but at home..."

"It'd be so easy to get lazy in the spiritual life," Massaglia finished. "Or get pulled away from it."

"Ah, I understand." Don Bosco nodded wisely. "You're right, and I'm glad you realize that. But your families are looking forward to having you back, so I want you to go for at least a month. Sound fair?"

Their anxious faces relaxed. "Sure does, Father!"

A month wasn't so bad, and they did want to see their families tremendously.

"I'll have great news to tell them," Massaglia speculated, beaming.

"You sure will!" cried Dominic. "Have you told the Sodality boys yet?"

"No. I was waiting for you to get to the meeting, but then I ended up blurting it out to you first."

"Well let's tell them!"

Dominic grabbed his friend's arm and raced off.

Moments later, Don Bosco heard a mighty roar from the little Sodality group and saw a pile of boys tackling Massaglia. Good thing he was a strong lad. They looked ready to kill him with love.

Did he know, that holy Saint John Bosco, that from the ranks of Dominic's humble Sodality, priests would issue forth like arrows from the string of an Archer? Did he foresee in his prophetic wisdom what those shouting, laughing boys would become — the pillars of a future Order of his, zealous shepherds of souls, bright lights of holiness?...that dashing, high-energy Cagliero would become a cardinal and the first Salesian missionary to Patagonia; that serious, ardent Rua would be venerated as a Servant of God; that Bonetti, Angelo, Vaschetti, and Bongiovanni would all become priests, bursting with love for souls? Perhaps he knew; perhaps not. And what of Dominic and Massaglia? Those two, the most promising of all: what would they become?

———————

"Did you hear the news?" Signora Carabella wrenched the sudsy water from a shirt and slanted up at her neighbor a look sparkling with gossip.

"I don't know, depends which news you're talking about," Signora Abruzzo answered primly.

"About the Savio boy, the one studying in Turin."

"Dominic? He's only been home about two weeks now, hasn't he?"

"Yes."

"I haven't heard anything, except that he's been telling stories to the children."

"Oh, and what stories!" Signora Carabella's eyes were wide with delight. "These aren't your normal yarns or fairy tales or even news from the city, oh no! He's been telling them about saints, martyrs, miracles, and all the rest of it!"

"And they listen?"

"Listen! My dear, they listen as if their lives depend on it! Even my Marco goes to listen, and he's Dominic's own age! And he's not the only one, either, mind you. He told me nearly all the boys Dominic used to play with will go and listen to his stories, even your own Luigi!"

"*Even!* And why can't my Luigi listen to holy stories? You act as if I've brought up a heathen!" Still, in the secrecy of her own mind, Signora Abruzzo was quite flabbergasted. "How does he get them all to come?" she demanded.

Signora Carabella threw up her hands, accidentally showering them both with dirty water. "How? Oh dear, pardon me! How? No one knows how! They just come! They just like to be around him, that's all! And when they come, he seizes his chance! His friend Angelo told my boy that Dominic has the same effect at the Oratory. According to him, the boys just love him and hang on to whatever he says. Mark my words, he'll be another Francis Xavier. Why, you should see the way those children are all of a sudden starting to pray at Mass. Nor is it just at Mass. Every time he goes to church, they come with him – Marco tells me he got a whole group of kids to go to Confession." She cocked a triumphant eye at Signora Abruzzo. "Your Luigi included."

Signora Abruzzo dropped her laundry into the wash pail and dropped her jaw almost as far.

"H...how?" she stammered.

Signora Carabella shrugged her shoulders and chuckled. "Bribed him."

"*Bribed* him! Dominic Savio *bribed* my son to go to Confession? How much did he give him?"

Signora Carabella almost tumbled into her washtub laughing. "A handful of nuts."

"What?! Don't tell me you're serious! I couldn't get him to go for a week of peach pies! And you're telling me he did it for a skimpy handful of nuts?" Signora Abruzzo was livid.

Her neighbor only smiled. "He did it for Dominic."

Luigi Abruzzo walked down the hot, dusty road, his hands shoved contentedly into his pockets. He'd never felt happier in his life. If he'd owned a pair of wings, he would have flown straight out of the universe for sheer joy.

Hearing running footsteps, he turned and found Bruno Vastelli and Angelo Savio sprinting to catch up with him. Now that was a strange pair. Good kids like Angelo didn't normally hang out with Vastelli if they could help it.

"Hey, Abruzzo! Where you going?" Vastelli called.

Abruzzo eyed him uncomfortably. He didn't really care to tell the village bully about this particular destination, but then, he supposed he shouldn't lie. Savio wouldn't.

"Church," he mumbled quickly, hoping Vastelli would mishear him.

Vastelli only grinned. "Same."

Abruzzo thought a tornado had hit him. "You — *what?!* I said I was going to church!"

"Yeah, and I said same."

Angelo almost died of laughter.

"What are you going to church for?" Abruzzo demanded, entirely befuddled.

"What are *you* going for?"

"I...I talked with Savio and –."

"Same."

Abruzzo stared so blankly that Angelo and Vastelli fell into another fit of hilarity.

"I heard him telling a story about Saint Ignatius and how he was a soldier," Vastelli explained, finding it fit to enlighten his bewildered companion, "and I kinda liked it, you know, the battles and bullet wound and all that. And when he – Saint Ignatius, I mean – asked himself why can't I be a saint, if other people have, I thought, now there's a logical question, and I might as well try this out. It was the way he said it – Savio, I mean. If Father Cugliero had said it, I probably wouldn't even have heard it in the first place. But Savio was so sure of it himself, and I like Savio. Ever since I beat him up about stealing the apricots and he took it like a man, I've liked him a lot. Well, anyway, I probably would've forgotten about Saint Ignatius the next day except that he and I – Savio, I mean – were playing ball with a bunch of fellows later on and he came up and asked if I'd go to Mass with him today. I couldn't really say no, 'cause...you know, and anyway, I remembered Saint Ignatius and thought, hey, why not? So here I am. And doing pretty well, too."

Abruzzo whistled so long the other two were surprised when he didn't drop into a faint. "That Savio's something else," he declared. "Here he's got you going to Mass and me resolved to go to Confession every two weeks, and neither of us would've done so for a million dollars without him."

"It's funny, though," Vastelli pondered. "I'm not doing it for him. I mean, he was the one who's getting me to go, of course, but the way he did it, he turned my attention on God, so I'm doing it for God, not for Savio, if that makes sense."

"Exactly," Abruzzo agreed. "That's the way it should be, and that's the way he wants it."

"What's he done for you, Angelo?" Vastelli asked roguishly.

"I couldn't finish telling you. But let's just say if I get to heaven, it's because of him. And I'll tell you what, we're not the only ones. Just ask the Oratory boys."

"We don't have to go that far," Vastelli replied, in the most subdued tone they'd ever heard him use. They had reached the village church, and Vastelli opened the door. "Just look inside."

When Dominic left for the Oratory in mid-August, his hometown of Mondonio felt it had lost its hero. The children and young people wandered about listlessly, clutching the medals and holy cards he had given them from the Oratory and wishing with all their hearts that their happy, lovable friend were back.

"Can you send me to the Or'tory?" little boys begged their mothers.

"Why, darling?"

"'Cause I wanna see Dominic."

Dominic himself was glad to be returning to Turin. Although he missed his home and family, the formation at the Oratory was like nothing he could get anywhere else, and he knew it. The farms sped by through the carriage windows, and he smiled at them in blithe anticipation. His old friends, the altar to Our Lady, the Saint Francis de Sales chapel, Don Bosco — all the people and places he loved most from the Oratory flitted through his mind as if waiting to welcome him back.

There passed the dear wooden sign marked "Torino" at the crossroad...there stood that big, funny rock...there were the city walls themselves! — a hoarse cry rang out from the gates. Dominic craned his neck to see what had happened, but nothing unusual met his gaze. Except that the driver had turned deathly pale.

They had reached the point where the carriage dropped him off, and now he was walking through the streets, growing more and more exuberant with each step. One street more...something about the city was strangely quiet, almost as if a heavy cloud hung over the walls. What was it? He didn't stop to think. There was the Oratory at last, his beloved, homely Oratory! He broke into a run.

A few minutes later he was sitting in front of Don Bosco, smiling all over his young face. How he had missed the saintly priest!

"How is everything, Father?"

They chatted a while. Then Don Bosco tapped his fingers matter-of-factly on his desk and looked steadily at the boy. "There's something you should know, son." His voice and face were calm. "The plague is back in Turin."

———————

It was cholera. The dreaded disease had been circling the globe for years, smiting utter terror and swift death upon town after town, country after country. Only a year ago it had raged furiously in Turin, wreaking horror and destruction. Now it was back. Once again people perished on the streets, when the day before they had been smiling and robust. Once again anguished mothers abandoned their diseased children and fled weeping, while the little ones shrieked in agony. Once again the death carts came rattling through the city, laden with dead, limp bodies, and carriages spun through the gates while frantic noblemen screamed, "Faster! Faster! Away!"

And once again, Don Bosco went fearlessly to work. Through the streets he marched, nursing the sick and administering the Sacraments to the dying, and with him went a group of Oratory boys, trembling but resolute.

Dominic begged permission to join this group, but Don Bosco was adamant. He was too young and too frail. He could pray, but that was all.

The death count rose higher and higher; the whole city seemed to be holding in its breath, waiting to see whom would be stricken next. Abrupt and horrible stomach pains, excessive vomiting, fierce muscle cramps, burning thirst, ashen skin: the symptoms followed one after the other until the sufferer became unrecognizable and died within days. The streets fell silent except for the terrified shrieks of the victims. Doors and stores were locked and double-locked. Normal life seemed to halt as if its clock had frozen in position. And still the death count rose, until its number became too oppressive to assess, and even that was lost in the dark void that had become existence in Turin.

And still Don Bosco and his boys strode through the streets like angels of hope and courage, while Dominic and his friends prayed in the Oratory chapel.

Life went on because it had to. Massaglia received the Roman collar and cassock, the boys who had gone home for the summer returned, and classes resumed. But ever in their ears were the rattling wheels of the death carts and the screams of the dying. If they managed to forget about the plague, it was never for long.

In the midst of this death scene, Dominic went about cheerful as ever, attacking his old friends with hugs the moment they set foot on campus and eagerly welcoming any new boys who came through the gates. Cagliero called him the "door-greeter." Little fellows who had lost their parents to the plague stepped with timid, desolate faces into the Oratory, and Dominic swooped on them and guarded them zealously until their fears were gone and their sadness dulled.

His prayer life continued to soar. Constantly, he prayed for his companions, his family, himself, and his purity. Constantly, he looked for and found ways to mortify himself. Constantly, he was living in the Presence of God. It became more and more frequent that someone would have to arouse him from prayer after he received Communion, lest he stay there interminably, lost in contemplation.

And thus, as the whole hardened, sin-ridden city of Turin stared with panic into the face of death, Dominic Savio was gazing with sheer love into the eyes of God.

————

A brisk October wind swept through the air, reddening the cheeks of a crowd of boys hard at play. Dominic shivered a little, then forgot the cold as a misshapen, threadbare ball came bouncing his way.

"Get it, Savio!" Bonetti yelled.

Dominic dived to grab it but was knocked over by a bigger kid and rolled over onto his back laughing in defeat.

"You're too skinny for this game," Bonetti grumbled, coming over to give him a hand.

"Oh? Watch me!"

Seizing Bonetti's hand, Dominic leapt up, then tore after the fellow with the ball and jumped on him with the intention of tackling him to the ground. The only result was that he dangled in the air, his arms wrapped around the other's neck, while the boys hollered in mirth.

"Nice try, Savio!" they shouted hilariously. "Way to teach him a lesson!"

From his considerably higher viewpoint, he noticed just what he was always on the lookout for. It took him a moment to gather enough willpower to break away from the fun, but through continual self-denial, such things had become habit to him.

"You win, Ballesio," he said, patting his prisoner on the back.

Then he dropped down and ran off towards the object of his attention.

The object of his attention was a thin, sickly-looking boy whom he had seen a few times before. The newcomer stood watching them with large, wistful eyes that began to sparkle with joyful surprise when Dominic approached.

"Hello! You're new here, I guess? What's your name?"

"Camillus Gavio."

"Gavio! Ha, I like that! I'm Savio! Dominic Savio."

Gavio smiled. "They seem to like you over there. See, they're watching us. Do you know all of them?"

"Oh, sure. It doesn't take long to know them." He waved an arm at them to signal that they should play without him. "Do you know anyone here yet?"

"No. I'm pretty sick, so I can't play the games, and lots of times I just don't have the energy to meet new people."

"That's too bad," Dominic frowned in honest concern. "What made you so sick?"

"It was palpitation of the heart. I almost died of it."

"Oh, no!"

"Yeah, I'm only just recovering now. I had a scholarship to study art and sculpting at the Schools of Turin, but since I got sick, they sent me here first to get better."

"Gee, I'm so sorry! I guess you must really want to get better, huh?"

"Well," Gavio answered meditatively, "not really. I only want the Will of God."

Dominic nearly flipped. His eyes round with delight, he cried, "Why, then, that means you must want to be a saint! Is that right?"

"Oh, yes. I've always wanted that."

Dominic shone. Gavio was smiling wider than he had in a long time.

"Tell you what," Dominic decided. "There's an inner circle of us here who want to be as holy as possible. We have a Sodality in honor of the Immaculate Conception. How about you join us, so we can grow holier together?"

"Why, of course!" Gavio cried. "What kind of things do you do to become holy?"

"Well, first of all, we try to become saints by being joyful. 'Serve the Lord with gladness' is our motto here at the Oratory. We also do our best to remain pure, in both big and small things, and we do our duties and prayers as well as we can." Suddenly he laughed hard. "Goodness, I sound just like Don Bosco!"

"That doesn't seem very hard or complicated," Gavio mused.

"It's not complicated," Dominic agreed, "but it can be hard. You see, it's easy enough to say, but lots of times when you get to it, a thing seems so small that it shouldn't matter, and then you say to yourself, 'I'll just skip this chance and wait for the next one.' But you really grow when you seize every chance you can, and that way, doing every little thing for God becomes a habit."

"I see," Gavio nodded. "I'll try my best to do that."

Let no chance go unseized. *Let no chance go unseized.*

Thus thought Camillus Gavio when, kneeling at prayer, his sickly frame felt faint with exertion. Thus he thought when the pain riveted through his body and he wordlessly offered it to the Triune God. When he had to overcome his shyness to speak up about his Lord at the Sodality meetings, "Let no chance go unseized" were the words that dispelled his hesitation.

And just as Dominic had promised, he surged in his ascent to holiness. Even the most devout boys looked up to him; the grave listlessness that had hung around his face gave way to a content and enduring smile; those in charge marveled at his virtues.

Meanwhile, Dominic, as usual, humbly had no idea that he'd had anything to do with this transformation. He exulted in having such a holy friend and continued to go about welcoming the new boarders, sending his wayward companions to Confession, praying for the end of the plague...

The disease raged on. Death after swift death struck the city. Night after night Don Bosco slumped into bed exhausted by his efforts to assist the dying. Dear God, there were so many of them! So many shrieking in agony, so many begging for the Sacraments after having led lives of unspeakable vice, so many who still refused to repent, so many children abruptly orphaned and left unprotected to the blasts of the criminal and poverty-stricken city. What could he do? He, one tired man...

In his dorm, Dominic knelt praying.

No, Don Bosco thought, he did not serve them alone. God reigned supreme. God had not forgotten them. Yet so often it felt as if He had forgotten — they were dying in sin out there even now, racked in torments and about to go to worse, and there were so many of them! If only he could stop it, or at least save one more —.

A knock sounded at his door.

"Who's there?" His voice was full of fatigue.

"It's me, Father. Dominic Savio. Please come quick!"

"What's wrong?"

"Please, Father, it's urgent! Bring everything you need to save a soul!"

Don Bosco hesitated a moment. It was late at night and he was utterly exhausted, but he had learned from experience to mind such compulsions from Dominic. He got out of bed and lit a lamp.

The streets were blanketed in darkness as he followed the boy in and out of obscure alleyways. Everywhere the moaning and wailing of plague victims met his ears, but Dominic did not stop for any of them. Growing awe took hold of the priest's heart as the lad hurried on through the hazy, dismal maze of the city, never stopping, sure as an arrow. There was no way Dominic could be finding his way all on his own.

Then all of a sudden the boy was racing up three steep flights of steps, while Don Bosco followed close behind. Yellow light peeked through uneven cracks around a door, and before this at last Dominic halted and knocked loudly.

"Here, Father."

Then he merely turned and left.

A pale, wide-eyed woman opened the door, cautiously, as if she were expecting a thief to force himself in. On finding Don Bosco there, she almost burst into tears of relief.

"Oh, thank God! Father," her voice cracked, "come in quick, please! My husband fell away from the Faith, but now he's dying and wants to return to it —."

Don Bosco needed no more. In a moment he was at the man's bedside, while the sufferer gasped out his confession with his last breaths. A few more moments and the man was dead in Don Bosco's arms.

The next day, as soon as he could, Don Bosco motioned Dominic aside.

"My son, how did you know that man needed the Sacraments?"

The lad's tranquil smile faded, as intense sadness crept over his countenance. He raised two reluctant eyes to the priest's, unable to speak, and Don Bosco noticed they glistened with tears.

He did not ask another word.

It happened again. This time Dominic was kneeling in the chapel, praying his heart out for two charges of his, Duina and Ratazzi. Antonio Duina had been entrusted to him by Don Bosco with the express instructions to teach him to read and write and the understood intention that Dominic make Duina a better Catholic. Ratazzi was a whole other deal.

The nephew of a renowned government minister, he had been the exasperation of those in charge of the Oratory since the day he stepped foot on campus. He was haughty, violent, and unruly – just the opposite of Dominic and just the type Dominic specifically targeted with his at-home missionary zeal. He had made it his determined goal to win Ratazzi over to Christ.

He was laying out his plan now and testing out scenarios for weak spots. It seemed to be sturdy enough. Now what he needed was a battalion of angels and a storm of grace. Bowing his head, he slipped into communion with God.

It happened very naturally, and though it had happened more times than he could count, he hadn't expected it in the least. As always, it seemed as if he were quite suddenly but very gently transported into a different universe. The sights that met his eyes were beautiful beyond description. Sweet Mary! – how dazzling with purity! – his heart reached out in ardent, yearning love. Nothing could keep him from this love – no, never – nothing but himself. Oh! Was there a word for this utter beauty? *Beautiful Mamma, help me! Keep me pure as you are pure! Death before sin, my Queen!*

She looked back at him with an affection so tender that it made his heart ache with devotion. For a long time they simply gazed into each other's eyes – or was it only a moment? Dominic had no way of knowing, nor did he think to wonder. He only knew that he loved her so much, and she loved him so much more...

Then she softly touched his cheek, spoke to him, and was gone.

He did not lose a minute. She had told him where to go, and he went.

Through the chapel doors, out the Oratory gates, up the ghastly, infected streets, down the even ghastlier alleyways; then there stood the house in front of him. He rang the bell.

What happened next was so human and so like Dominic that it is amusing and moving at the same time, as stories of the saints often are.

A man opened the door, and Dominic asked if someone inside were suffering from the plague. The man said no. Dominic insisted. Perplexed, the man assured him that no one inside had the plague.

Then Dominic stepped back and with a puzzled face surveyed the front of the house. "But..." he murmured, "but I'm quite sure..." He regained his confidence. "Yes, this is the house. Won't you please take a look around, Signor? I'm certain that there's someone here who needs our help."

There lies the touching sincerity of Dominic's love. Like many an uncertain teenager, he may have doubted himself, but he never for a moment doubted Our Lady. Thus, he thought he could have mistaken the house, but that there was a plague victim in the building she had shown him was not even a question.

The houseowner could not resist the boy's earnest plea. Good-willed though a bit doubtful, he turned into the house, promising to search the place as best he could. His wife would probably think he was losing his mind, but after all, it couldn't hurt. He'd just get this over with and then send the good lad away reassured. The man poked his head behind the sofa, flipped up a long tablecloth and peered underneath, surveyed the guest room. Goodness, he hadn't seen that dusty little book in years. He blew it off and would have opened the cover except that the boy was in such a hurry it would have been rude. What on earth was driving him? They left the room and opened a closet across the hall.

Suddenly the owner staggered against the wall, blanched of every trace of color. A filthy pile of rags was huddled up in the far corner, unnaturally blue and stinking horrendously. It was human.

He saw immediately the deep sockets around the eyes and heard the staggered gasps of pain, and he knew at once that this was a victim of the plague. He tried to speak, but the muscles in his mouth couldn't even move; all he could do was stare in horror and pant hoarsely for breath.

Beside him, the boy knelt down and addressed the dying woman with the same grave courtesy he would have used for the Mother of God. "Signora, would you like a priest?"

She could only muster the slightest nod, but her eyes were desperate with the desire. Already she was gulping up her last breaths of air.

The priest arrived in time. With an expression like that of a child comforted by its mother, the woman passed into eternity with a perfectly clean soul.

Meanwhile, Dominic went back to the Oratory and commenced praying for the conversions of Duina and Ratazzi.

Duina was more difficult than Dominic had anticipated. The first lesson they had, he swore the whole way through. Dominic had plenty of common sense, and that common sense advised him to bite his lips and keep silent, but the words caused him physical pain. If they hurt him, he thought grimly, what must they do to Jesus? But now was not the time to remonstrate.

"This is how you make the letter 'C,'" he explained calmly, after an especially violent outburst. "Like a circle but not the whole way. Try it."

Duina flung down his chalk, shattering it to smithereens, and buried his face in his arms. "It won't work! Mine never turn out right, and they never will! I'm too stupid!"

"Oh, come, Duina, *you're* not stupid, though it would be pretty stupid *of you* if you gave up before trying." Dominic handed him a new piece of chalk. "And if you would, please don't throw this one, 'cause it's the last one I have."

Duina snatched it with a nasty glare. "Then go get more."

That stung. Dominic felt like slapping him, but just in time he remembered that every humiliation could be turned into a gift to offer his Jesus, and his anger evaporated. He smiled broadly at Duina.

Duina stared back in bewilderment, then bent over his slate with more diligence than he had ever shown.

"There!" Dominic cried, when Duina showed him a perfectly round 'C.' "I knew you could do it!" Duina grinned sheepishly. "See, you're smarter than you think. Ready for the next one?"

"Guess so."

Dominic took the chalk and slowly demonstrated how to draw a 'D,' but Duina was no longer paying attention. His eyes were fixed curiously on Dominic's face, avidly searching for something that would tell him what made this boy rejoice when he had been insulted and spend tireless energy helping a person who swore at him. What was it?

Unable to figure it out, he looked back down, and when he noticed the 'D' and realized he had no inkling how to write one, he cursed horribly. Dominic said nothing, only closed his eyes and moved his lips.

And all of a sudden, Duina understood.

"What do you do when you're walking through the city?" Gavio asked. "All the bad images..."

Dominic shuddered. "I don't look up."

"He just looks at our feet so he knows where to go," Cagliero explained roguishly.

"That's it!" Dominic agreed. "Highly recommend."

"Have you ever bumped into a pole?" Massaglia questioned with a grin.

"Oh, once or twice, when you fellows didn't have the charity to warn me."

"Well, what if we were all looking at each other's feet?" Massaglia returned innocently.

"Then it's a mercy we ever found the Oratory!" Dominic retorted, laughing heartily.

"Did you hear there's been another Grigio sighting?" Cagliero asked.

"No?"

"Don Bosco was in some shady back-alley of the city bringing the Sacraments to a dying person, and there were two thieves who tried to kill him, the disgusting brutes –."

"Easy, Cagliero, you're in seminary! Set an example for the rest of us!"

"All right then, the lovable benefactors, and anyway, being lovable benefactors, they were about to kill him, you know – Don Bosco, who feeds, houses, clothes us, and teaches us to speak kindly of our enemies – they were about to *kill him*, when Grigio appeared out of nowhere and saved the day!"

"Aww, come on, what did he *do*?" the boys protested. "Tell us what he did!"

"He barked and growled and scared them out of their wits. Apparently he leapt on one, and the poor lovable benefactor begged Don Bosco for mercy until Father called the dog off him."

"That dog isn't any normal dog," Angelo declared with conviction.

"He definitely isn't," Dominic concurred. "He only shows up when Don Bosco's in trouble, and then no one ever sees him otherwise –." At that moment his eyes glazed over, and he caught his breath and fell silent.

"What's up, Dom?" Angelo asked.

There was no response. Dominic's whole countenance radiated with rapt adoration as he gazed intensely ahead of him. He seemed frozen in space; then, in an abrupt motion, he turned and left their company.

Uneasily, the boys tossed wondering glances at each other. They had seen it happen before, but they weren't sure what it was about.

"You ask him later," Cagliero whispered to Massaglia. "He tells you the most."

"I'm not going to tell you if it's his secret."

"You're right. Don't. But just look at him: everything about him is so intent, and he's already not very strong. Sometimes I wonder if it'll –." He broke off, visibly upset, and didn't finish.

"God wouldn't do that," Massaglia said gently.

Cagliero looked at him. "I don't know, Massaglia, I just don't know." He glanced through blurred eyes at his young friend and whispered, "He looks as if he's already in heaven." Then he added in a voice so low it was almost inaudible: "And he's ready."

————

It was several days before Massaglia could muster up the courage to ask. Meanwhile Dominic had gone into ecstasy again in front of his friends, this time in the middle of class. It came out very timidly when Massaglia finally did ask the question.

"Savio, why do you sometimes just stop and walk away in the middle of our games or conversations?"

Dominic turned red. For a while he didn't know what to say, then he answered rather embarrassedly, "I see such beautiful things, Massaglia — heaven becomes opened in front of my eyes, and then...well...I have to go away because I get scared I'll say something ridiculous in front of my friends."

Massaglia felt a strange lump in his throat, but it wasn't one of sadness. Yes, the saints were human. Every single one of them had been. And it was such a human answer.

———

Sundays at the Oratory were wonderful. Several hundred boys from the streets would crowd into the packed grounds for the catechism and games which Don Bosco held every week without fail. They were quite the lively and colorful crowd, and thus Dominic flew into their midst like an arrow.

His tried and almost consistently true method of fishing Turin boys went something like this:

Questionable kid on left side of field; Dominic on right. Game goes on and Dominic observes mannerism of questionable kid from afar; ball whizzes toward Dominic and he pretends to dodge but gets himself hit. Dominic moves to left side of field and starts making small talk with questionable kid to sound the waters; if the water seems to be the right depth, Dominic gradually shifts the conversation to questionable kid's faith while still testing the waters. Then, with a prayer, *plop!* goes the fishing line, and Dominic says casually, "So, since we're talking about it, how about going to Confession with me this Saturday?"

"This Saturday? Gee, that's sooner than I'd like, but far away enough,

I guess — look out, ball's coming your way!"

"You'll come, then?"

"Fine, fine, if you'd like."

Dominic wasn't clueless enough to leave it at that. When Saturday came around, he'd hunt down questionable kid, who'd turn bright red at seeing him, and would cart him off to Don Bosco (with suaveness, of course). Then questionable kid would come out of the confessional a few minutes later as happy kid. Many times happy kid would be so happy that he would go frequently to the Sacraments for the rest of his life.

As Don Bosco commented, "Savio catches more souls with his nuts and games than many priests do with their homilies."

It was on a particular Sunday in December that Dominic ran about hard at play and missionary work and entirely in his glory. The plague was fading out at last, Christmas was around the corner, and an animated mood of hope and exuberance hung about the Oratory. The gloom of terror and stark uncertainty that had clung to the wild youngsters had finally stolen away, leaving them wilder than ever. Dominic skimmed about, bubbling over with joy and largely contributing to the infectious vitality, as the cool wind whirled playfully about his ears.

"Hey there, Dadamo! Wanna come to Mass with me tomorrow?"

"Only you could make me! I'll be there!"

Dominic cheered loudly and ran to Mamma Margaret. "Mamma, do you have any nuts I could borrow?" he wheedled sweetly.

"Just how does one borrow nuts?" the good woman demanded, unable to keep down a broad smile.

"You'll get your pay in heaven."

"Ha! If all the boys said that, the pantry would be clean empty in twenty minutes!" Her warm dark eyes twinkled at him as she poured a generous pile of nuts into his cupped hands. She knew exactly what would happen next.

Dominic whirled back outside, yelling at the top of his lungs. "Anyone want some nuts?"

Free food was the love, dream, and motto of the Turin boys. They stormed him until Cagliero forced his way through to establish himself as bodyguard and make sure they didn't suffocate him.

"Ok, ok!" Dominic was laughing, as the sea of faces jostled to get closer to him. "Morindo, you can have them if you tell me what's so bad about mortal sin."

Morindo, a juvenile criminal, paused, torn between fierce craving and hesitant perplexity.

"Yeah, what *is* so bad about it?" one kid demanded.

"You're smart," another scoffed. "It hurts people. Obviously killing someone is bad."

"Hey, be quiet!" someone called. "Let Morindo answer!"

"But why is killing someone bad?" Morindo was thinking aloud. He looked in confusion at Dominic, who smiled and pointed up. "Ah, I got it!" Morindo shouted. "It offends God! I see now! Even if no one else knows and no one else sees..." his voice trailed off to a whisper as another light flicked on in his soul, "it still offends God, doesn't it?" He stared at Dominic, wide-eyed and trembling with remorse.

"You're exactly right, Morindo," Dominic answered softly, pouring the nuts into his hands. "Hey, fellas! Three cheers for Morindo!"

As the boys whooped and yelled, Morindo broke into a slow grin, tossed the nuts into his mouth, and after a moment of hesitation and a nudge from Dominic, charged off toward the confessional.

Dominic hollered for joy. Ratazzi, who had watched the whole thing, was smirking at him, but that was something to offer up. Besides, Ratazzi's turn was coming up soon, God willing.

Spilling over with energy, Dominic raced back toward the crowd, when Bonetti came flying toward him, his face frantic and aghast.

"Savio! Savio! Come quick!"

At the note of terror in his voice, a black curtain seemed to drop over Dominic's sky.

"What is it, Bonetti?" he asked quickly.

"Gavio!" Bonetti wept. "Camillus Gavio. He's had a relapse, and they rushed him to the hospital. Oh, Savio, he was so good and inspiring! He's barely been here a month, and already I feel I couldn't do without him —."

"No!" Dominic clutched Bonetti's wrist. "Is it that bad?"

"I don't know!" Bonetti sobbed. "He looked awful, but he can't — dear God, don't let him! He was so pale and weak, I could hardly bear to watch, and...and..." He gasped for breath. "Oh, Savio, they gave him two weeks left!"

"Sweet Jesus!" Dominic moaned, as a sword plunged through his heart. "I need to go to the hospital. Which ward is he?"

"Second. He wants to see you in the worst way, but the hospital's closing to guests in less than an hour."

Dominic's face was stricken with pain as he answered: "I'll run."

The romping crowd of boys with all their laughter and competition faded away into a blurred cloud as he dashed forward, clinging to faith, blinded by tears. His friend. Dear God, dear *God!* His friend was dying.

———

Antonio Duina watched as a knot of lads gingerly placed a card on a growing card tower. It was quite a feat of architecture. Idly, he leaned his cheek on his fist and stretched his legs toward the snapping fire. Maybe if they kept building it...

He groaned and sat up straight, then slumped down again.

"Everything all right?" one of the boys inquired.

Duina nodded.

To be honest, though, something was terribly off kilter in him, and he wasn't sure what it was, and he was too afraid to find out. He kept thinking of Savio, and every time he did, he felt acutely restless. It was a running Savio that kept appearing before his mind, a Savio so determined and running so hard that the whole world assembled against him wouldn't be capable of stopping him. And here was he, Duina, sitting. Yes, something was wrong.

He had run off late that evening, with a face so tenacious and intently sincere that Duina had frozen in position and simply stared at him. There was an air of genuine joy about Dominic that always made Duina want to dart up and talk with him whenever he saw him, but this time he had known he couldn't. Dominic was running; he was going somewhere and it was urgent. And here was he, Duina, sitting.

If only he could run, too, maybe the burning knife racking his insides would go away; but there it was, twisting horribly, that awful blade of discontent that craved for something infinitely tremendous but never seemed able to find it. As an almost-illiterate brick apprentice, he had once imagined that learning would satisfy that immense hunger. But now that he was studying, he knew better. He also knew that whatever it was, Dominic had it. Dominic had it and he didn't, and that was why Dominic was running and he was sitting, why Dominic was happy and he was excruciatingly restless –.

The door banged shut against the whistling wind, and Dominic entered, scraping his shoes on the mat in the doorway. At his arrival, the whole atmosphere of the room brightened.

"Your dinner's here, Savio!" Duina called to him, over the friendly welcome of the boys.

"Why, thanks, Duina!"

Pushing to Dominic the dinner he had been entrusted to guard for him, Duina added wryly, "It's probably cold by now."

Dominic said grace and tasted it. "Sure is."

His voice was cheerful but Duina noticed that his face was more tired and serious than usual.

"Anything wrong? Where were you?"

There was a pause, then Dominic sighed very deeply. "Camillus Gavio is...is dying, Duina. I went to the hospital to visit him, but it was closed when I got there."

Duina knew well how close Dominic was with Gavio, and he was rather surprised at the calmness with which his friend spoke. But when he glanced up again, he found such terrible, heavy sadness in the other's eyes that he had to look away.

"I'm sorry, Savio," he awkwardly murmured.

"Thanks, Duina," Dominic smiled at him gratefully.

Perhaps it was that gentle smile. Perhaps it was the constant example of a living saint that Duina had before him every day. Perhaps it was the thought that if he had been in Dominic's place, he would have wanted to possess a heart huge enough to run to a frail, easily forgotten, dying kid as if the whole world depended on it, even though he'd have to leave the fun and games, even though he knew that the doors might be shut when he got there, even though it meant eating cold soup afterwards. Perhaps it was all of these, or perhaps it was something entirely different, that caused Duina to abruptly realize what would fulfill his restlessness and to crack open his soul to God's grace.

Whatever it was, he was no longer sitting. He was walking, jogging — no, he was sprinting at breakneck speed — right toward the open doors of the chapel.

"I'm so afraid, Savio."

Dominic fought back his tears. "You've loved Him and given Him everything, Gavio," he said, placing a cool cloth on his friend's brow with the gentlest of hands. "Don't be afraid."

"I haven't done enough," Gavio murmured.

"Dear Gavio." Dominic had to turn away to hide the tears that were creeping unbidden down his cheeks. "I know He'll welcome you to heaven. He measures your effort, not your success, and you've been trying so, so hard."

Gavio smiled weakly at him, then his face contorted as pain shot through his body.

He had been sent back to the Oratory from the hospital, not because he was better but because he wanted to die there. He knew it was any day now. Racked with grief, Dominic spent every spare moment at his side, nursing him, consoling him, and praying with him. If their friendship had been strong before, it was doubly so now. Suffering and preparation for the hour of death had rendered the bond between them imperishable.

Gavio relaxed at Dominic's words, but Dominic left the sickroom in an agony of empathy. His was a sensitive soul, so finely attuned to others' emotions and so easily cut to shreds by their pain. To watch one of his closest friends so quickly and surely dying was for him a kind of deep and real martyrdom.

A hard whirl of exhaustion beat through his head as he walked toward the dining hall. He had been taking care of Gavio for so many long and draining hours that now he could scarcely drag his legs forward. If only his tortured mind could forget that stare of helpless fear in Gavio's eyes!

"Hey, Savio!" a voice called.

It was Ratazzi. Dominic did his best to greet him cheerfully, but he could barely force the words out of his mouth.

Ratazzi was in a dark mood. "That sniveling pipsqueak of a Gavio is still hanging on and causing everyone trouble, huh? He's sure pretty selfish, demanding all your attention like that."

Dominic spun on him hotly. "You stop that right now. I help him because he's my friend, not because he makes me, and you know that!"

"Sure, sure," Ratazzi jeered. "You just say that because you wanna sound like a little saint. No one could actually care about such a loser."

They had reached the dining hall by now, and a group of boys who had come early for supper were lounging at the tables. In indignance, they perked up their ears at Ratazzi's comment, for they all respected Gavio and were sincerely worried about him.

"You take that back, Ratazzi!" Dominic raised his voice fearlessly. "I won't have my friend talked about like that!"

Possessed by sudden fury, Ratazzi drew back his fist and punched Dominic in the mouth.

Already weighed down by fatigue, Dominic completely forgot all the prayers, sacrifices, and efforts he had been making for Ratazzi's conversion. He never had done anything by halves. That included the ringing blow he dealt in return to a stunned Ratazzi.

They rolled around kicking on the ground until the onlooking boys realized Dominic would soon get beat to pulp by the bigger, stronger Ratazzi and rushed forward to break up the fight. The moment they grabbed hold of him, Dominic felt crushed with remorse. Everything he had been doing for

Ratazzi — and now!

"God forgive me!" he moaned, and rushed blindly into the chapel.

He stayed there for a long time. Tenderly, softly, the Presence of God enveloped him, and his soul settled into its characteristic peace. At last he got up, and it was with an untroubled smile that he returned to the dining hall and offered an apologetic hand to Ratazzi.

The latter refused to even look at him, but Dominic took the snub with tranquil humility.

A moment later, Angelo rushed into the room, his face white, and whispered something to Dominic. Dominic instantly flung his soul into fierce, agonized prayer. Gavio's last hour had come.

———————

The evening passed by in a haze, with doctors rushing to and fro and calling out indiscernible, urgent orders and boys running in throngs to kneel by Gavio's door. Steady, murmured chanting broken by crying filled the corridors as the youths lifted their schoolmate's soul to God. Time ceased to exist as they waited...and waited...and waited...

At last a heavy silence fell upon the Oratory when the doctors admitted there was nothing left they could do. The boys began the prayers for the dying.

It was with tears in his eyes that Dominic begged Don Bosco to let him stay by Gavio's side, but the priest gently refused. When the boys finished the prayers for the dying, they were sent to bed, and Dominic with them.

Yet could he have slept that night? Nay, he must have prayed the whole night, in spirit never left his friend's side, battled with him to the very threshold of heaven and defended him with every grace he could obtain against the final tempests of the evil one. But we do not know for sure. All we know is that when he was told the next morning that his companion was dead, he quietly asked permission to see the body, and it was granted.

He entered the sickroom where he had so often cared for and chatted with his buddy; he saw the pale, limp body lying motionless upon the bed and wreathed in a tender smile of peacefulness; he clasped the cold hand for the last time, and with tears running openly down his cheeks, he whispered in a strangled voice: "Farewell, Gavio. I am quite sure that you have gone to Heaven, so prepare a place for me there. However, I will always be your friend and will pray for the repose of your soul as long as I am left here on earth."

Then he left to arrange prayers and Communions to be offered for the soul of his departed friend.

———————

Ratazzi, as usual, was in a terrible mood. He hated the Oratory, he hated his lofty government minister uncle for sending him here, and above all, he hated Don Bosco. He was sick of the place.

Glowering with anger, he scooped up a ball of slush and packed it tight between two clenched hands. Softly, he cracked open the door of the Oratory and hurled the snowball at one of his friends.

"Hey, there!" someone yelled. "Cut it out! Don Bosco says no snowballing inside!"

Ratazzi smirked. Screw Don Bosco. That was exactly why he was doing it. Darkly rebellious, he whizzed another snowball against the wall. Then Dominic appeared in the doorway.

"Come on, Ratazzi," he admonished mildly. "You know better."

That was it. Don Bosco's stupid little minion. He'd show him. Ratazzi stormed up and sent Dominic a smarting blow.

"There!" he screamed. "Now go tell Don Bosco!"

The boys caught their breaths, wondering if Dominic would strike back like last time. For the smallest fraction of a second, Dominic struggled with himself. Then he simply turned away.

Something hit Ratazzi as if Dominic had given him a physical blow. But it wasn't physical. It was something more startling, more reeling than anything he'd ever felt in all his years of brawls. Doggedly, he fixed his eyes on Dominic's back, but it was more of a keen scrutiny than a glare. The next moment he had spun around and left, with some obstinate trace of a swagger that still clung to its old but now shaken pride.

Inside, the boys rallied indignantly around Dominic, insisting that he tell Don Bosco what had happened.

"He won't stop hurting you if you don't get Don Bosco to put an end to it," Bonetti urged.

"He shouldn't even be here," Rua shook his head. "He's always throwing the place into chaos."

"Go tell Don Bosco," Angelo begged him. "Please, Dom, he oughta know."

Dominic only shook his head. "Thanks for your concern, fellows, but I can't do that."

No, he couldn't – it would ruin so much. He had already gotten into a fight with the kid, and then to tell on him would be too much. No one liked that. No, he would simply let it go.

Angelo and Bonetti glanced at each other in moved helplessness. Impulsively, of the same accord, they got up and withdrew into an empty hallway.

"Why is it so easy for him?" Bonetti demanded, a bit emotionally. "It seems to be natural for him to turn the other cheek. Me – I'd have picked Ratazzi up and punted him across that field!"

"It's not easy for him," Angelo said, grinning at the image of a catapulting Ratazzi. "He just works on self-control so hard and so often that he can pull that kind of coolness off. Trust me, Bonetti, he's always been working on controlling his temper. He's not a born saint like some people think."

"Maybe," Bonetti returned dubiously. "But he is a saint."

Angelo laughed. "I won't argue that. But my point is, it's serious effort on his part and lots of grace on God's part that make him that way. Not lucky genes."

"If you hadn't grown up with him, I wouldn't believe you."

"I wouldn't blame you. Gee, he inspires me so much."

"He just makes me want to be a saint, you know? Just seeing him – I can't even explain it – something in me starts aching with the desire to love

God as he does, but then I try, and...oh, I don't know. He's so far ahead of me, and I know I can never be like him, but I still want so much to be holy like that!"

Angelo bent his head ponderously to one side, as the memory of a certain conversation flicked through his mind. He understood now. Sainthood really wasn't about catching up to Dominic Savio.

"I know exactly what you mean," he finally answered. "I once said the same thing to Dominic, how he seemed almost perfect and I was always slipping into trouble. You know what he said? Any good he ever did was because Our Lady helped him. You're right, Bonetti, we are so helpless on our own. But so is Dominic. It's God and Our Lady who make us saints, not ourselves, and if they can make a saint of Dominic, they can make saints of us, too."

Meanwhile, Ratazzi had stumbled against a cold brick wall and was clutching his pounding temples. What was happening to him? Why was he shaking like this? Why couldn't he get that image of Dominic turning away *out* of his stupid head? Arghhh – was it – *was* God real? No, no, of course not – but then what was this intensity all around him –.

"Ratazzi!" one of his friends yelled. "Where are you?"

The boy ducked out of his hiding place. He would forget about it, or figure it out later. Now was time for fun.

But the blow on Dominic's nose still tingled around his knuckles. He couldn't forget, the questions wouldn't leave...

Years later, Ratazzi visited the Oratory as a Minister of the Royal Household, a highly successful and deeply devout Catholic man.

As he chatted casually with one of the priests who had once been his classmate, the topic of their boyhood friend Savio came up. Ratazzi's face grew fond and grave, and he retold the story of how Dominic had simply turned away when he struck him.

"I've heard many powerful homilies, especially from Don Bosco," he confided humbly. "But no homily I've ever heard since then, either in or out of the Oratory, has ever done me as much good as Savio's example that day."

Seven

Dominic walked briskly through the crowded streets toward one of the magnificent churches of Turin. It was freezing cold. A few flakes of snow wandered through the air, driven by a stinging wind. He hastened his steps. If he hurried, he'd get out of the cold faster. Then he stopped short. If he slowed down, he'd stay in the cold longer. That was something to offer up. A brief sigh escaped his lips. Then he smiled ruefully and shook his head toward heaven in playful affection, as he moved on at a much slower pace.

Despite the thickness of his warm coat, he felt like an iceberg when he reached the church. He entered through the tall doors, then again stopped short. Someone was loitering there at the entrance. Sharply, he turned around and approached him, a blue-faced ragamuffin dressed in threadbare clothing.

"Hello, there!"

"Hello."

"Like to come to Mass?"

The boy shrugged. "Not today."

"Why not? It's warmer in there."

"I'll bet. But, you see..." He flushed a brilliant red and dropped off in the middle of his sentence.

"What's up?" Dominic persisted kindly.

The boy was pressing himself stiff against the wall. At the empathetic tone in Dominic's voice, he looked up with trust-filled eyes. "It's a bit awkward you know," he began, grinning, "but my pants has a big tear in the back. I couldn't go in like that."

"I see, true enough. That's an easy fix, though!" Dominic slipped out of his coat, grinning back at him. "You take this. It's nice and big and oughta cover up your tear quite nicely." He helped the fellow's numb limbs into the sleeves. "There. Don't you look great!"

"Gee, thanks! Boy, it's warm, too! But wait, how about you now —."

"Never mind, let's go in. We're already late."

The way back to the Oratory was bitterly cold. Dominic whistled hymns and kept his eyes down from the sordid city sights as usual. He could voluntarily keep his eyes pure, but his ears — that was a different matter. Sometimes he wished he could shut them as easily as he could his eyes. The cursing was everywhere, and he was physically hurt by it. What must his Jesus feel, he moaned inwardly?

A well-dressed gentleman in front of him dropped a package into the gutter and broke into a volley of blasphemies. Dominic caught his breath as pain flashed through his body, pain that, as Don Bosco would record, would prove to seriously affect his health. Lifting his cap, Dominic murmured, "Praised be the Name of Jesus Christ!" He paused at the sense of a familiar whisper in his heart. He really didn't want to...but no, he could not let this one pass. An ignorant street boy was one matter, but a sophisticated, elderly gentleman? *All right then, Gentle Mary. It's a Friday, so this one will be for you, in honor of your Seven Sorrows.* He took a deep breath, and with that resolute chin set firmly in courage, walked up to the man.

"Excuse me, Signor! Could you do me a favor?"

"What is it?" the man asked a bit curtly, still disgruntled.

"Could you tell me how to get to the Oratory?"

The gentleman's features relaxed. "I don't know where that is, son."

"That's all right." The gentleman was right at the mood Dominic had been aiming to get him. Here went. "Could you do me a different favor, then?"

"I sure could. What do you want?"

Dominic edged closer to him and lowered his voice so that only the gentleman could hear him. "Could you avoid taking the Lord's Name in vain next time you're upset?"

The man's eyes bulged. He fumbled for an oath adequate for expressing his disbelief but for once in his life couldn't find one. Dominic watched him, unconsciously braced in suspense.

"Well, I never!" the man finally gulped out. His goggling eyes took on a scrutiny of admiration. "You're right, my young friend. This is a terrible habit I've slipped into, and I'll do my best to break it right away. How's that?"

Dominic's chest heaved in colossal relief. "That's wonderful, Signor! Thank you!"

"Thank *you*, my friend."

Bright red chilblains had erupted on his hands by the time he reached the Oratory and sat down for class. There were 153 boarders now, and Don Bosco had accordingly been able to open up classes on campus for some of the boys. Because of his declining health, Dominic had been one of the first chosen to attend these, to spare him from the trip to and from school in the city.

He opened up his books and took out a pen as the teacher began his lecture. His body was still numb from that walk without his coat. His head ached from the violent strife against impurity he fought every time he went out into the city; his neurons still shot pain from the countless blasphemies he had heard. He felt a bit dizzy. Well, that was no matter. Contemplatively, he studied his chilblains and began to prick them deliberately with his pen nib. There, that was better. The longer they stayed around, the longer he'd have to offer them up.

Glancing up, he found the eyes of one of his classmates riveted on him in horror and had to choke to cover up his laughter.

Yes, Dominic was one of those blessed individuals who could suffer and still be happy. In fact, when he suffered, he was especially happy, because he knew it was a chance to love his Savior, to throw into that infinite debt of the Cross some miniscule token of appreciation.

He was so happy that when one of the boys started making faces behind the teacher's back, he couldn't contain his laughter. His seminarian friend Michael Rua was teaching the class and wheeled around to demand who had caused the disruption.

"I'm sorry, that was me," Dominic apologized, his shoulders still shaking.

A moment later, the boy impishly twisted his face into another grimace. The whole class began to grin watching Dominic struggle to stuff down his mirth until finally, as he gasped up for air, all the pent-up joy burst out in a long, hard peal of laughter.

"Dominic!" Rua snapped.

But Dominic was gone. His sides were aching; try though he did, he could not stop the laughing. Now his classmates were starting to snicker along with him.

Peeved, Rua ordered him to kneel in the middle of the room until the end of class. Meekly, still trembling blithely, he knelt down, and the lesson continued. His chilblains were smarting acutely.

At the end of class, his friend Vaschetti came over to tease him about his case of the giggles and noticed Dominic's red, inflamed hands.

"Gee, Savio, those chilblains look awful!"

"Thanks, Vaschetti!" Dominic answered appreciatively, slinging his arm over his companion's shoulder as they left the classroom. "I find that the bigger they are, the better it is for my health."

Vaschetti snorted. "You're a nutjob."

———

Dominic's love for penance, as can be inferred from the above incident, had in no way diminished over time. He and a handful of his Sodality friends had formed a habit of eating the crusts of bread which the other boys threw away, then giving up their regular meals. As Don Bosco wryly put it, Dominic was "economical to a degree."

But Dominic's body was taxed, unable to keep up with his

gargantuan spirit. One icy morning in the January of 1856, Don Bosco noticed that the boy was unusually pale and sent him to bed.

Dominic went cheerfully, but Don Bosco was starting to feel concerned. He had kept Dominic at the Oratory for classes, but he still looked frail as ever. Of course, he still played with all his normal gusto and hunted down penances like a gold miner, but the good priest suspected that was part of the problem. If he kept pushing himself so relentlessly... Don Bosco smiled as he remembered the boy's enthusiastic request for a hairshirt. What a gem of a soul! But he'd have to monitor those penances more closely from now on.

Don Bosco was making his usual inspection of the Oratory when he reached Dominic's dorm and dropped in to inquire how the lad was feeling.

"Do you need anything, Dominic?"

"I'm fine, Father, thank you!"

"Are you sure? No water or extra blankets –?" Don Bosco broke off in blank dismay. Was he really – where was –? "Dominic!" he cried in exasperation. "Don't tell me you've been lying in this North Pole of a room with that one single sheet to cover you!"

"I...have."

"I – you – how long have you been sleeping with only one blanket?"

Dominic blushed. "Since the summer, Father."

Don Bosco clutched his head in agitation. "And I suppose in the summer you slept with ten, eh?" he conjectured grimly. "My dear boy, do you want to die of the cold?"

"Oh, I won't die of the cold!" Dominic assured him confidently. "Besides, in the stable at Bethlehem and on the Cross, our poor Lord had even less to cover Him."

That was the last straw. In unquestionably clear terms, Don Bosco entirely forbade Dominic from any kind of penance whatsoever, unless he received express permission.

A few minutes later, Dominic's dejected face was poking out from beneath a pile of quilts.

———

Before long, Dominic was back on his feet again, but it was quite a troubled head that those feet carried around. How on earth could he become a saint if he wasn't allowed to do penances?! All the saints did penances — why, his patron saint Dominic de Guzman had flogged himself! Poking chilblains was nothing compared to that. He slumped down on a bench and buried his chin in his hands. Dear Mamma, tell him what to do! The *Imitation of Christ* said you had to do penance to overcome your will, and *obviously* to align your will with God's you had to overcome it, first. He pulled at his nose in perplexity. He'd never encountered such an immense obstacle in his life. Of course, he knew Don Bosco wanted him to get to Heaven, but then how —?

Fortunately, Don Bosco found him just then, and being Don Bosco, he immediately knew something was wrong.

"Why so gloomy-looking, Dominic?"

"I don't know how to become a saint if I can't do penance." The boy's bluish eyes looked up at him with a hint of reproval.

"Ah, Dominic." The priest sat next to him on the bench. "I'll tell you what. Obedience is the penance God asks of you at this time in your life. Obey, and I promise you that will make up for all the penances you would have done."

"All right," Dominic acquiesced reluctantly. "But you're sure that's all you'll let me do?"

"The only penance I'll let you do is bear patiently whatever God sends you — heat, cold, illness, blows, insults, and so on."

A disappointed sigh escaped the boy's lips. "But Father, I have to put up with those anyway!"

"Exactly. But if you suffer them graciously, you'll grow in virtue and earn merit in God's eyes. That's what you're looking for, isn't it?"

"Yes...but I won't be able to earn enough merit if I'm not doing more..."

"Ask for God's mercy, then. If you were to try to earn sainthood, Dominic, you'd never get it. It's a gift from God that you must ask for unceasingly. Trust that He will give it to you in His goodness, and in the meantime try your hardest to be perfect — *but.*" Don Bosco's eyes twinkled. "Without doing penance."

"He will give it to me," Dominic repeated under his breath. "All right, Don Bosco, I'll go for it."

"That's my boy."

He will give it to me in His goodness. How often he had stopped to wonder, nagged by doubt, how his young, insignificant self could become a towering monument of holiness like those saints he so admired. He, Dominic Savio, a mere teenager who'd never even stepped foot outside his country, who'd never been seized by pagans and commanded at swordpoint to deny the Christian God, who'd never fasted for days on end in a cold hermitage — how could he become a missionary, a martyr, a saint as he so longed? How, when he was only thirteen years old and lame as a drowning duck?

And here, at last, was his answer. *He will give it to me in His goodness.* Yes, God saw his efforts, He knew his flaming desire, and He saw that even if Dominic were to convert the whole world, even if he were to suffer the most excruciating martyrdom for the sake of His Holy Name, even if he were to never let food pass his lips and kneel unceasingly in prayer, still the eternal gap between Creator and creature, Savior and saved, God and man could never be filled. The saints had not been able to fill it either; not even the Blessed Mother, God's perfect human, could satisfy that yawning chasm of debt. One Man alone could fill it. The Man Whose Body had ripped on the nails of the Cross — the Man Whose Love was eternal, Who Himself was eternal — He alone could swell through that eternal void between Dominic and God, between Dominic and sainthood. Dominic could try, and it was entirely necessary that he did try as hard as he possibly could, but alone even his fiercest efforts amounted to absolutely nothing. God alone could make him a saint. And God, in His everlasting goodness, would do it.

The sea of Oratory boys crammed around Don Bosco, yelling and beating a drumroll on the rocking floor. A jumble of beloved names were flung into the air, caught up and shouted with relish, then forgotten to the sway of another cry.

"Do you want to hear the winners or no?" one of the seminarians bawled over them, grinning.

The boys sent up a shattering roar.

"Quiet, then!" The seminarian rolled his eyes in mock despair.

"The winners of the popularity contest!" Don Bosco thundered. "Third place: Seminarian Giovanni Cagliero! Second place: Dominic Savio!" The room threatened to collapse under the stomping, shrieking, and whistling, as the boys caught up Cagliero and Dominic on their shoulders and almost dropped them in their enthusiasm. "And first place is Seminarian Michael Rua..."

Dominic tried not to let his popularity victory get to his head. He couldn't help but notice, however, that several of the rougher kids paid him more respect because of it. Therefore, he made the most logical move a Christian in that position would make and doubled down on his missionary action.

"Whoa, there, Tom!" A passionate young swearer was cut short in his sentence. "I wanna show you something. Follow me!"

The intrigued Tom abandoned his friends and ran at the heels of the older boy, giddily flattered that the second most popular boy in the Oratory should single him out.

"What is it? What is it?"

Dominic twisted and turned around corners and down hallways, while his suspense-bound companion grew more impatiently curious by the second. Then a halt, a twinkle in Dominic's eye, a final turn — and Tom's face went blank. The chapel!

"What...about...the chapel?" the deflated youngster asked blandly.

"Why, Tom, you sound so disappointed!" Dominic rebuked, valiantly keeping a straight face. "Confession's a wonderful —."

"Confession?!!" poor Tom squawked, jumping as if he had stepped on a porcupine.

"Yeah, my friend. You swore, didn't you? Go on, Don Bosco won't die of horror. He's heard that one before."

"Awwwwwww, Savio..."

———————

But Dominic used his accepted leadership to defend and not just revive the purity of his friends.

One gusty afternoon, when the Oratory was packed with street boys drawn by the Sunday catechism lessons, games, and food, a glinting-eyed man slipped through the gates. He was dressed in a gaudy suit of red and had all the appearances of a circus performer, thus drawing an expectant circle of lads around him within moments.

"Like to hear a story?" he offered. There was an air of mystery in his demeanor.

"Yes! Yes!" they chorused, wide-eyed with curiosity.

"Well, then. Have a seat. Once upon a time..."

His silvery voice and dramatic expressions captured their attention, and his jokes tickled their sense of humor. Drawn by their roars of merriment, more and more boys left their games to sprawl themselves down at the perimeter of the audience.

Bonetti found his way there and soon felt his sides were cracking. Gee, he didn't even have space to breathe! Vaschetti next to him was whacking him on the back and rolling around in the grass. Then all of a sudden the two boys had frozen in position, staring uneasily at each other. What they had just heard was wrong. Don Bosco never would have stood for it. They glanced around. A few of the boys seemed dubious, but most had ignored it. The man wouldn't say anything like that again, Bonetti was sure... Another joke sent the boys howling, followed by a second subtle mockery of their Faith. The two friends exchanged disillusioned glances.

"I'm out," Vaschetti muttered in disgust.

They got up and left.

Every now and then another courageous lad stood up and walked away from the increasingly blatant blasphemies, but several more were joining unaware. Finding himself unchallenged, the performer slowly stripped himself of all reserve and unleashed a volley of insults toward the Catholic Church, priests and religious, long-held dogmas, the Blessed Virgin, and God Himself.

More left. Others came flocking — the street boys who only came to the Oratory on Sundays and to whom religion mattered little, unformed and unaware of the sacred Christian mysteries as they were — they settled themselves on the brown wintry grass and listened undisturbed, several even laughing.

Into this scene entered Dominic. He loved a good laugh as much as anyone. Emphasis on *good*. It took him five seconds to figure out the man's evil intent, and in five seconds his audacious clarion call to arms was ringing over the awakening heads of the boys.

"Come on, don't sit around listening to this guy! He's out to destroy your souls!"

There was a tangible hush. Then the boys began to murmur.

"He's right!"

"Yeah, we don't wanna listen to this nonsense."

"Let's go play ball!"

"I'm glad someone said something."

"Three cheers for Savio!"

Headed by the fearless young frame of Dominic Savio, the crowd of boys pushed away from the stunned performer. Feebly, the man opened his mouth to call them back, but the words lodged fast in his throat. He glanced around desperately. Not one person had remained to listen to him. Mortified, he pulled his hat low over his forehead and slunk hastily into the streets. The Oratory never saw him again.

It was this kind of missionary spirit, this unflinching, undying zeal for souls, that magnetized Dominic's heart toward the missionary saints and inspired in him a strong desire to become one. Keenly perceiving as he was, however, he realized he didn't need to travel into the middle of obscurity to obtain his goal. He would start right at home: his dream was to become a priest and teach catechism to the clueless village children of Mondonio.

He and Massaglia spoke of their vocations often together. Already a seminarian, Massaglia gave him all kinds of insights into clerical life.

"It's strange, isn't it, figuring out what your future's meant to be?" Dominic mused once.

"Yeah, sure is a big thing to think about. But then, God guides your career and vocation as much as He does your first baby steps, so I guess it's not so scary after all."

"You're right, Massaglia," Dominic laughed. "I like that!"

Then one evening a speaker visited the Oratory. He wore a pair of burning dark eyes and spoke in a bit of an accent assumed by years away from Italy. There was nothing particularly extraordinary about this simple, forthright priest, but his message opened a whole pleading country before the gaze of Dominic's missionary heart.

England.

Don Bosco had had a marked passion for the conversion of England ever since the renowned John Henry Newman from Oxford had become Catholic ten years prior. In the effort to compile a definite history of Anglicanism, Newman and several other scholars had reached the unexpected conclusion that only Catholicism could be the true religion. Now the intellectuals of England were writhing under the powerful pen of their once-adored Newman, while Don Bosco begged his boys to pray for the salvation of souls in that country.

And now this humble, little-known missionary, Father Lorenzo Gastaldi, was standing before Dominic, describing to the lad's pounding heart the droves of English scholars struggling with the truth and at last accepting it, the agony of souls clinging to the vanishing conviction that they had always possessed reality but now glimpsing it in all its terrible splendor.

In a swift throbbing of compassion, Dominic abandoned the thought of Mondonio. He would go to England. He would help them find that beautiful Truth, which animated and sanctified every moment of his life – oh! poor, suffering country! He would pray hard for those shaken, searching souls.

Pray hard he did. He thought of England and prayed for England and received Communion for England, just as he did for certain boys at the Oratory who especially needed it. And then, in an unheralded moment of grace, God responded.

Dominic was making his thanksgiving after Holy Communion, when a wide plain blanketed in mist stretched out before his eyes. A large multitude was wandering in confusion on the plain, looking for something and unable to find it.

A voice, sweet with the language of Heaven, told Dominic: "This is England."

Then he noticed the Holy Father, Pope Pius IX, resplendent in his pontifical attire and bearing a bright torch. As the Pope approached the crowd, the mist rolled away, and the people found themselves surrounded in light.

"This torch," the voice spoke again, "is the Catholic Faith, which will illuminate England."

Two years later, at the prior request of Dominic, Don Bosco related the vision to Pope Pius IX, whose eyes grew intent with amazement.

"What you tell me," the Holy Father confided, "confirms my resolve to do everything possible for the salvation of England. This has been a special care of mine for a long time." His eyes wandered musingly out the window into the hard blue Roman sky. "What you have told me is, at the very least, the counsel of a devout soul."

"Hey, Savio!"

Dominic halted in the middle of an all-out chase, panting heavily. "What's up?"

Cagliero pointed to a scowling boy walking into the yard.

"There's a new fellow who — whoa!" he caught Dominic's arm as the younger boy swayed dangerously. "You all right there, Savio? What just happened?"

Dominic brushed it off. "Oh, I'm fine. Just a bit dizzy from running."

He was still unsteady on his feet. Not convinced at all, Cagliero led him to a bench and sat him down. He searched Dominic's face, his pulse quickening with unspoken dread.

"The new kid?" Dominic prodded.

Cagliero gave him a look. "His name's Celestine Durando. Don Bosco's asking us, the Imperial Guard, to give him special care."

"Oh?" Dominic smiled.

He loved helping the new boys who needed "special care" from the Imperial Guard. That was code for: "here's a rough character come into the Oratory, and you good fellows need to help him become a saint." Don Bosco, like Dominic, was very strategic in his evangelization.

"He sure looks annoyed," Dominic observed, watching Durando loiter at the outskirts of the games.

"Well, we're not sure he wants to be here."

"Why not?"

"I don't know."

"Let's ask him." Dominic jumped up. "Hey! Durando!" The boy turned. "Welcome to the Oratory! I'm Dominic Savio, and this is Giovanni Cagliero. I'm a student, he's in seminary."

"You're gonna become a priest then, huh?" Durando asked Cagliero scornfully.

"I am, God willing."

"Ugh, I *hate* priests!" The lad's eyes burned with hard, passionate fury. "So hypocritical and judgmental and –."

"Hold *on!*" cried Dominic. "Maybe you think so, but don't go talking like that about God's holy servants, and especially in front of my friend!"

"Oh, no? I'll teach you to tell me how to talk!" Durando struck Dominic across the face and kicked him in the shin. "Take that!"

Dominic went an angry red. The hot-headed Cagliero barely restrained himself from tackling the punk before he remembered he was a seminarian.

Taking a deep, somewhat shaky breath, Dominic looked his opponent in the eye. He waited until his emotions were mastered, then said firmly, "You did wrong, but I forgive you. But," he added wryly, "I wouldn't try that behavior on other people."

———————

Dominic was walking through the city again. As usual, the filthy words that struck his ears sent bullets of pain through his body.

"My poor, poor Jesus," he murmured with heartbroken reverence. "May Thy Sweet Name be praised."

Something hard and unrelenting was squeezing at his lungs, denying him a full breath of air. He furrowed his brows. He had felt this before on several occasions, though he couldn't remember when it had started. A few months ago, maybe? He struggled to fill his lungs, but the effort only made them feel more compressed. Frustrated, he tried again. He'd go insane if he couldn't get a deep breath — but he couldn't. His chest had never been so tight. A slight stone of dread sank into his stomach. For weeks and weeks he had been quite confident that the pain would go away, for after all, he had always had some kind of physical ailment to offer up. But now he was second-guessing himself. A faint shadow was stealing slowly over his bright assuredness. Was it possible that... He lifted two wide, anxious blue eyes to the matching sky. O Blessed Jesus! He would trust in his beloved Lord! Yes, he would trust Him in anything, no matter what strange or unexpected things He willed. But was it possible that —?

A light cascade of bells interrupted his thoughts. Ah! Fearful notions dissolved under the clear music as Dominic dropped to his knees. Here was Purity Itself passing through this waste of corruption!

Within a few seconds, two altar boys appeared, ringing the bells to herald the coming of God and King among His people. Directly behind them came the priest, vested and bearing the Blessed Sacrament, perhaps returning from a sick visit. The sky had been gushing torrents of April rain earlier that morning, leaving the pavement warped with grimy puddles. Blissfully unconcerned, Dominic was plunged on his knees an inch thick into the mud, gazing toward his Lord. But another man stood close by — stood — while the

Uncaused Cause, Truth Itself, the Divine and Eternal Creator of the Cosmos passed by. Dominic looked up. The man was a young, well-built soldier, dressed smartly in a crisp, impeccable uniform. The street was disgusting.

Humbly, gravely, Dominic drew out his handkerchief and spread it out on the ground beside him. With a little smile, he glanced at the soldier and motioned toward the cloth.

There was a moment of confusion as the soldier returned the gesture with a questioning expression. Then he comprehended. Meekly ignoring the handkerchief, he blushed and knelt down right where he was, in the middle of the mud and grime.

Yes, Dominic was a veteran at ruining nice, clean trousers, a champion at gently bending stiff knees in allegiance to his Master.

His Master, passing by in veiled Majesty, saw, and His Heart was touched. When the priest disappeared and Dominic stood up, he found that his lungs were no longer tight, and he breathed a deep, deep breath of air.

———

"Durando's converted," Cagliero announced.

"What!"

"Celestine Durando, the fellow who hated priests and socked you in the cheek."

"Yes?"

"He's converted now. He met with Don Bosco a few times and decided priests aren't so bad after all, and now he wants to join our Sodality."

Dominic whistled. "God works *fast*! That kid only came here two weeks ago!"

"Eh," Cagliero shrugged. "What else would you expect when he's in the care of a priest who's a saint?"

"Good point. Did you tell him about Sodality?"

"He's going to the meeting tomorrow."

"Wow." Tucking a ball under his arm, Dominic grinned and shook his head. "That Don Bosco. I wish I could be like him."

"Don't we all."

"Here comes Massaglia. Let's play ball. Hey! Massaglia! Bet you can't catch me!"

Amazing, he thought, as he tore off with the wind. Amazing how one priest could transform so many lives. Just looking around, face after happy face met his eyes as a testament to the saintly leadership of that man Don Bosco. What a man! If only he could become a priest as soon as possible, how arduously he would work for the salvation of young souls, as did Don Bosco! How he longed to set the torch of Christ blazing around the world, in Italy, in England −. His chest had become unbearably tight again. He slowed to a halt, his cheeks unnaturally bright, and flung himself into a gasping heap on the ground.

"Savio!" cried Massaglia. "Are you all right?"

"I...I don't know."

"Does something hurt?" Cagliero demanded, anxiously scanning his face.

"I can't breathe. I...think I'll be okay." He fought for air as his fingers clutched the grass. "It happens a lot."

"You don't look okay," Massaglia doubted, shaking his head. "C'mon, Dom, let's go to Don Bosco. He'll know what to do."

He wrapped a secure arm around his friend to help him up.

"Can we go to the chapel instead?" Dominic begged.

"Don Bosco should know," Cagliero faltered.

"I know, but I want to tell *Him* about it first."

Massaglia looked down quickly at an unexpected catch in the boy's voice. For the first time in his life, he found a hint of fear in Dominic's eyes.

A wild rush of stunned, desperate, defiant words almost choked Massaglia as they surged to his lips, but something stilled them powerfully. His heart in his throat, he bowed his head and said, "Of course, Savio."

"Thanks, Massaglia."

The three of them spent a long time in the chapel. Though Massaglia and Cagliero tried heroically to focus their attention on the Tabernacle, they found their eyes darting back to Dominic time and time again. The lad's brows were knit, his eyes closed tightly, his lips moving slightly, tensely absorbed in prayer. Yet they noticed that as time went on, his features relaxed and his frame sank into the pew until his body was resting at ease. His lips fell motionless, his face was uplifted, almost glowing, and the two onlookers felt as if they were looking on the countenance of an angel.

When they left the chapel, the dinner bell was ringing. Dominic's breathing was back to normal. At first his friends didn't know what to say, but Dominic, who always knew exactly how to handle an awkward silence, jumped right into carefree conversation.

"God is so good! So Durando doesn't hate priests at all now? It's not just Don Bosco he likes?"

"Well, he likes me now," Cagliero chuckled.

"That does say a lot," Massaglia jabbed him.

Their laughter rang over the field, and the two seminarians decided in relief that their younger friend's sudden illness must have been a passing scare.

As they neared the dining hall, however, Dominic casually mentioned, "It's May next week."

"The month of Our Lady," Massaglia smiled. "Doing anything special?"

"Oh, yes. I want to make this May especially special for her."

"Especially special!" Cagliero teased. "Why so special?"

Dominic's expression was so authentically tranquil and his voice so very low that neither youth grasped the meaning of his reply. "Because I think..." he answered softly, "I think it will be my last."

Eight

Don Bosco looked at the slight form of the boy before him with a sense of sinking dread. Dominic had lost weight. His features were serene and happy as usual, but any observant person could tell he had grown weaker. He could no longer keep up with the other boys in their games; Mamma Margaret had reported he barely finished his food. Dear God! the priest moaned silently. Please do something! Perhaps Massaglia and Cagliero could be easily reassured, but Don Bosco had given Last Rites to too many of his boys – but no! No, not that! Oh, God, don't make it that! Besides, Dominic had been sick several times and had always gotten over it. Yet try though he might to push the frigid thought away, Don Bosco couldn't help but sense that this illness was different.

"Good morning, Father!"

Dear boy, he was cheerful as ever.

"What's on your mind, Dominic?"

"I want to do something very special for Our Lady this May. What should it be?"

"Be exact in your duties."

"All right. But..."

"You want to do more, eh?" Don Bosco grinned. The boy hadn't changed a tad.

"Yes."

"Well, all right then. Receive Holy Communion every day."

"I already do," Dominic reminded him humbly.

"You do, don't you." Don Bosco leaned back in his chair and stared at the ceiling. "Hmm. How about you tell someone a story about Our Lady every day?"

"Sure, I can do that! And what special grace should I ask her for?"

Earnestly, Don Bosco looked into the boy's eyes and answered, "Ask her for the graces to become more pleasing in the sight of God and to become healthy again."

Dominic's face grew grave and thoughtful as he studied the rough wooden floor for a moment. Then he lifted his eyes to Don Bosco's and replied, "Yes, I'll ask her for the grace to become a saint. And I'll also ask her to help me in the last moment of my life, that I die a holy death."

He was never morbid or gloomy, however. If he experienced pain, few around him ever knew it.

As for the month of May, he started telling stories of Our Lady as soon as the first day of the month arrived.

"Hey, Savio, why do you care so much?" one uninterested listener scoffed, the first time he tried.

Dominic promptly lost his temper. "Why do I care!? Only because your souls were paid for with God's own Life! Only because as friends we oughta be helping each other get to Heaven, *eternal happiness*! Only because God *says* to go out and save souls! That's why I care — is that enough for you?"

"Yes, go on with the story."

They glanced at each other and burst out laughing.

As day by day slipped by, Dominic's love for his Queen soared to the very heavens as he strove to give her anything and everything that came his way. And the Lovely Virgin, never outdone in generosity, flooded him with consolations to bolster him for the trials ahead. So frequently did he fall into sweet ecstasy that Don Bosco remarked he was more often in the world of angels than with his companions at the Oratory. And the more lavishly Mary bestowed her graces on him, the more ardently and gratefully he made little acts of love back to her.

"Gee, Savio!" his buddy Giuseppe Reano speculated one day. "If you're doing so much for the Holy Mother this May, what will you be able to add for her next May?"

"Hm," Dominic reflected. "Well, Reano, you just let me take care of that. I've got to do everything I can now, and if I'm still around next May, you can ask me again then."

A thunder roll of scattered *thuds* echoed through the chapel as the boys dropped the kneelers and knelt for Mass. Close to the front, Durando studied every object on the altar and every motion of Don Bosco and the altar servers. He'd like to be an altar server, he thought. Funny, he mused, less than a month ago he'd hated Catholicism and priests with a passion. He'd been so angry when his parents sent him to the Oratory. And just look at him now! He was so much happier now, and he had wonderful friends like Savio, Cagliero, and Don Bosco to look up to and imitate. Dear God! Thanks a lot for Don Bosco! What would have happened to him without that holy priest? He'd probably have ended up in jail. Instead – at that moment, Don Bosco lifted up the Host, and the bells pealed forth in exuberance. Durando looked up at his God; something spoke to an unsounded depth in his heart; he started, then froze. Good God! He was meant to become a priest! He, Celestine Durando, who a month ago would have cursed at seeing one! He trembled, gasped, sank back weakly, still staring with wild, rising delight at the serene Eucharist. He, of all people, a priest! A minister of God, to transform bread and wine into the Divine Body and Blood with these very hands! A surge of intense gratitude swept from the core of his heart.

"Yes!" he murmured, awestruck. "If You choose me, Lord, despite my utter unworthiness, then the only answer I can possibly give You is yes!

Yes, yes, yes!"

The minutes crept by unmissed. Then came the time for Don Bosco to distribute Communion.

In those days the priest would say Mass in front of the altar with his back to the congregation. Few people would receive Communion more than twice a year. Those who did would kneel at the altar rail, and the priest would come to them and give them the Eucharist. Don Bosco, however, encouraged his boys to receive Communion often, in some cases even daily, knowing the power of this greatest Sacrament.

On this bright morning in May, he turned from the altar, expecting to see a crowd of youths waiting at the altar rail in honor of Our Lady. His face fell. Not one boy was there. Smitten with disappointment, he turned back and continued with the Mass.

Durando noticed his discouragement, as did several other boys. Right away his mind set to work. It couldn't happen again, he determined, that Don Bosco should be so disappointed and the waiting King in the Eucharist so neglected. The boys would have to coordinate with each other who received when so that the altar rail would never again be left empty.

The first person to whom he suggested his idea was Dominic.

"Durando, you're a genius!" the lad enthusiastically slapped him on the back. "We'll call it the Communion Club!"

"I like it, Savio, I like it! Any idea when we should start it?"

"Why, today! Massaglia! Wanna be in our club?"

The Communion Club took off. Morning after morning, Don Bosco turned from the altar to find a prayerful line of boys kneeling in anticipation to receive their Lord. Sundays, feastdays, humdrum weekdays — not one was missed by that faithful cohort of young soldiers.

Don Bosco's heart was touched. When he moved along the crowded altar rail, his eyes glowed upon each lad's countenance. When he placed the Host upon tongue after tongue, his hand trembled with stirred emotion. When he returned to the altar with an empty ciborium, it was all he could do to keep from washing it with his own tears. His boys were drawing close to their God.

It was on such a morning that he knelt in the sacristy after Mass to make his thanksgiving. From the reception of his own Communion, his focus drifted to that of his sons'. What more could he ask but that they unite themselves to Christ in such a profound manner as the Eucharist? From there their holiness would flow. Temptations may assail, but girded with the shining white armor that was that delicate Host...

A voice broke his thoughts. Someone was still in the church, talking, it seemed, with another person. Surely the boys knew better than that, or perhaps something had gone wrong. Standing up from his kneeler, Don Bosco left the sacristy and peered into the dimly lit chapel.

"Yes, my dear Lord," the voice spoke, then fell silent, as if listening to a response.

Ah, Lord! Don Bosco bowed his head in moved reverence. Yes, he knew that voice. There the boy knelt, near the spot where he had received Communion, only closer to the Tabernacle, his visage smitten with loving adoration.

"Yes, oh my God!" he cried softly, clearly. "Yes, I have said it before and I say it again: I love You! And I will love You to my last breath! If You see that I should ever hurt You, let me die before I can. Oh my God! Yes! Death before sin!"

Death before sin. So drastic to our lax minds, yet nothing makes more sense. What else should fall from the lips of the true Christian? We who authentically love Him should be willing to suffer anything rather than hurt Him. Thus the startling battle cry of Dominic Savio is only an echo of the song of the Church, for so rang the testimony of the martyrs.

Silently, Don Bosco turned back into the sacristy. This was the love his young people were capable of, he marveled, if they received that greatest of Sacraments with sincerity.

———————

Dominic's plea was answered.

A serene evening rested over Turin, dusky with the approaching summer light. A few stars faintly specked the tender purple heaven. Below in the city, drunkards shrieked with coarse laughter, and scenes of obscenity took place on almost every block which wrenched sobs from the hearts of forgotten guardian angels. But farther away from the noise and degradation, near the outskirts of town, stood the haven of sweet chastity from which warm light thrust its rays through the windows like beams from a lighthouse in a storm. Through these windows one could see a crowd of boys, pressed close in a circle around a cassocked priest, who sat smiling at them, answering their questions, and speaking to them, with gestures of his hands.

They were speaking of purity.

"Father," one curly-haired lad wondered, "is it better to be familiar with evil things so we can know when they come and protect ourselves against them, or not know of them at all and be less likely to commit them?"

"Ah, Tommaso, very good question. It is better to remain innocent. If you don't know of a certain sin, you can't be tempted to commit it, now, can you? The less you know and think of sordid things, the more your mind can rest on God in His perfect purity. That's why you must be very careful about what you hear and see."

"It's pretty hard, Don Bosco," another fellow sighed. "There's bad stuff all around us."

"I know, my boy." Don Bosco met his gaze with deep empathy. "We Christians have always been the sore thumb of the world, haven't we? Standing out by standing up for purity. But let's not look at it from the world's side, because we're not of this world. Let's look at it from God's perspective. Think of Mary, who was perfectly pure. What happened to her at the end of her life? Yes, Marcellino?"

"She went right to heaven, body and soul."

"She did," Don Bosco nodded. He looked around at the intent faces surrounding him. Dominic's eyes were locked on him, and his countenance was almost glowing. "And it makes sense, doesn't it, that a body that never once committed sin should not be left to corrupt in the ground? If death is a result of Original Sin, and Mary never had any sin at all on her soul, then logically she could not die. As for us, the more we keep ourselves pure, the more fit we'll be to have eternal life in heaven. So think of the reward, boys, when the struggle for your chastity and innocence is difficult. Do you remember what the reward is?"

"A good conscience."

"Heaven!"

"The respect of others."

"Stronger love and a pure heart to give to the woman you marry."

"Deeper love for God."

"Sainthood, maybe."

"Better protection against temptations and the habit of overcoming them when they come."

One boy grinned. "If you beat the temptation and Mamma Margaret finds out, she'll give you a hot roll."

Don Bosco and the boys roared with laughter.

"Dominic," the priest asked, noticing the youth's smile still had its radiance about it, "what are you thinking about the reward given to the pure?"

"'Blessed are the pure of heart,'" he quoted simply, "'for they shall see God.'"

"See, my boys," Don Bosco went on, "this is why Confession is so important. When we wash ourselves in the Mercy of God, our hearts become clean, and we're able to receive these wonderful gifts you spoke of. Think of the delights of heaven: of having every desire perfectly fulfilled, of never having sadness or pain again, of seeing God Face to face, of beholding the Virgin Mary in all her beauty and splendor, of befriending the saints as you befriend each other now, only on a far deeper level, of being in each other's company forever, never having to part. Think of the end of time, when our bodies, like Mary's, will join our souls in heaven and we'll be able to touch with these very fingers the Wounds which bled to save us! Is it so terrible a price, after all, to look away from unchaste sights in the streets? To refrain from coarse language? To confess our sins when we fall?"

Some of the boys were blushing and hanging their heads; others had an unwelcome tear or two which was hastily brushed onto their sleeves; others glared darkly at the priest or pretended to look bored while their consciences writhed; others were shining with deep, Christian joy.

Dominic was one of these. His face was suffused with rapture and his body stood motionless. His eyes shone intensely with a loving gratitude beyond human description, as he gazed on something so real and so gorgeous that the rest of the room faded away to him, like mist before the morning sun. Stronger, and stronger, pulsed the rhythm of his soul — fiercer, and fiercer, it strained toward its Beloved — until, at last, he could bear no more. The cord snapped. He plunged into oblivion. His body sank back gently into the swift arms of Massaglia.

The tumult had subsided. From upstairs floated the quick commands of Mamma Margaret herding the flock to bed. Dominic's eyelids drooped slowly open.

"He's coming back," Massaglia announced quietly. "Your cup of water worked nicely, Cagliero."

Dominic opened his eyes. He was still lying supported by Massaglia, who was now kneeling on the floor. Don Bosco crouched nearby, his anxious gaze fixed on the boy's pale face. When Dominic managed a dim smile, he stood up reassured. Rua, Cagliero, and a few of his other close friends surrounded them, but the rest of the room was empty.

"Are you all right, Savio?" Cagliero asked in a low voice.

"Yes. Thanks for wetting me." Dominic plucked at his soaked shirt and grimaced.

They laughed, largely in relief.

"Any day," Cagliero offered generously.

"Can you sit up?" Massaglia questioned.

"I think so."

Slowly, Massaglia helped him up and brought him to a chair.

"What happened, Savio?" he asked tenderly, searching the younger boy's face with the concern of a brother.

The abstract gaze of profound gratitude returned to Dominic's face.

"He outdid my wildest hopes," he replied, his voice awed with humility. "I will never be tempted against purity again."

"See you, Massaglia! Have a great time with your family!"

"Thanks, Savio! Goodbye!"

The two boys clasped hands warmly and looked frankly into each other's eyes.

"Don't forget to pray for me," Massaglia bade.

"Every day — you know it." Dominic smiled at him with that meaningful glance of friendship. "And don't you forget about me, either."

"As if I could."

The carriage pulled off, leaving Dominic a waving speck, until the brick buildings swallowed both the Oratory and Massaglia's best friend from view.

How strange, Massaglia mused, what had happened the other night. Protection from temptations against purity. It had never been easy for Dominic to keep his heart pure. Massaglia knew it for a fact. Others quickly assumed that Dominic found it a piece of cake to turn from unchaste images and to keep his thoughts clean. Massaglia, however, had seen the whiteness of Dominic's knuckles as they walked through the streets together. He had witnessed the expressions of bitter struggle evident in his friend's face when temptation smote with fury. He had heard the low groans of discouragement, watched the innumerable sacrifices made for holy purity, and been present during hours of ardent, pleading prayer for that virtue. And Dominic had told him outright, as his closest friend. The temptations against purity were no less hard or real for Dominic than they were for the rest of the boys.

Only he had overcome them. Not *once* had Massaglia seen Dominic's eyes linger on an impure sight once he knew it was there. It had been his uncompromising dedication to purity, clung to through blood, tears, prayers, and built-up will power that had allowed Dominic to form habits which became instincts. Even then he had never grown relaxed. His guard was ever vigilant. He had truly been ready to die before committing one mortal sin, and

God saw. And God rewarded.

What a grace to long for! Massaglia thought. Protection from temptations against purity. It was one of those wishful ideas one thought of almost wryly when temptations assailed hardest, yet here his own friend actually had it. Saint Thomas Aquinas had been granted that grace, he remembered, as had a rare few other saints. And here Savio had it...

His shoulders shook with chills as he stared at his hand, still warm with the grasp of Dominic's firm handshake. Could it be that this hand had touched a saint's? That the so deeply familiar name of Dominic Savio would one day be inscribed in the canon of saints, treasured in the rich memory of the Church, called upon by the faithful down through the ages? Massaglia stared blankly at the houses and crowds that jolted quickly by. There stood the palace of the governor, a man famous and feared throughout the city and its surrounding area. But would the name of this man one day vanish while Dominic's lived on bright and loved?

It seemed that it would be so.

And if Savio could become a saint, then why not he, who had been created by the same Maker? Reverently, Massaglia made the Sign of the Cross and began to pray.

———

"Letter for you, Savio."

"Thanks, Bonetti!"

Dominic turned over the envelope and found Massaglia's name scrawled out in his familiar hand.

"Thank God!" he muttered under his breath. "I was getting worried about him."

He tore open the envelope, his heart warming to the well-known writing of his friend. Right away his heart missed a beat.

My dear friend,

When I left the Oratory, I thought I'd only be away for a short time, so I didn't think I needed to bring any books or school things with me. But now it seems my recovery will take time, and in fact, my illness is quite uncertain. The doctor says I'm improving, but I think I'm gradually getting worse: we'll see who's right. My worst regret is that I have to be away from the Oratory and from you, and that I've had to give up most of the pious exercises we used to practice. My only consolation is in remembering the days when we went to Holy Communion together, and the preparation we used to make for them.

However, although we're separated physically, we will remain united in heart and spirit. I want to ask you to get from my desk some manuscripts and the Latin copy of The Imitation of Christ, which is beside them, and send them to me. You can imagine how tired I am of doing nothing. The doctor won't hear of my studying at all. I have plenty of time for thinking, and I often wonder if I'm to be cured, or go back to the Oratory, or if this is to be my last illness. In any case, I feel ready to submit with joy to the Holy Will of God.

If you have any suggestions for me, tell me. Don't forget to pray for me, and if we cannot enjoy our old friendship, I trust we will one day enjoy together a happy eternity.

Remember me to all my friends, especially to the Sodality of Our Immaculate Lady.

Believe me,

Your affectionate friend,

Giovanni Massaglia

Dominic looked up from the letter into the cobalt sky. His entire being was shocked into silence. Massaglia...dying.

He had left for home because of a sickness everyone had believed would be brief and mild. Massaglia, who was strong as an ox and alive as a youth could be — how? Why? What had happened? His best friend...

Slowly, he sat down against the wall of the Oratory and stared absently into space. Something like a calm sea was rippling gently in his soul. A sea of tears, perhaps; but if so, tranquil ones; he was not upset. Somehow, he had not been hurled into confusion, grief, and desperate hope as when

Camillus Gavio had fallen ill. Why...he did not move a muscle when he realized why, but his breath suddenly seemed keenly deeper. He was on his way home, too, and that was why he did not fear losing Massaglia. He was near the end as well; they would not be parted long. A long, shaky breath escaped his lips. He was not afraid, only...only it was a tremendous thing to think on. Heaven – the object of joyful longing for every Christian – it was so near.

A jumble of shouts brought his attention back to earth. Rumor had circulated that Massaglia had sent a letter, and a troop of lads were running toward Dominic, demanding to hear the news. After an unusual period of silence on Massaglia's part, the Oratory had begun to wonder about him with concern.

"How is he, Savio?"

"Still alive, at least, I see."

"He says..." Dominic faltered. "I don't know how to say this."

They fell quiet. Gravely, they scanned his face and instinctively put their arms around each other's shoulders as they knew to do when times got hard.

"Tell us, Savio. What's up?" Angelo squeezed his shoulder slightly.

Dominic held open the letter for the circle of bent heads to read.

"He won't be back for a long time, longer than we thought. He thinks he might not come back at all, because...because..." His voice cracked a little. "He might be dying."

"Good God!" a boy groaned softly. "Don't take Massaglia!"

They looked at each other seriously. Cagliero, standing next to Dominic, began to pray, and one by one they joined him, their arms still locked in strength.

"Hail Mary, full of grace... Hail Mary, full of grace... spare him, dear Mother. Bring him back to us... pray for us sinners, now and at the hour of our death."

When they finished, there was a long silence. At last Vaschetti spoke up.

"He's a strong fellow. I'm sure he'll pull through."

Giuseppe Momo nodded confidently. "The doctor says he's better, too."

"We'll keep him in our prayers," Angelo asserted. "I'm sure God must want him to live. He's such a holy, likeable person — he'd win so many souls if he could finish seminary and become a priest."

Dominic said nothing.

———————

My dear Massaglia,

Your letter reassured us because it showed you were at least alive, which we were beginning to doubt. We didn't know whether to be glad or sorrowful. I've sent the things you asked for. I'll only add that though Thomas a Kempis[1] is a good friend, he is dead and gone; you must search for him in his writings, and bring his advice to life by putting it into practice.

I see you miss the opportunities we have here to make spiritual exercises. You're right. When I'm away from the Oratory, I feel the same need. I used to try making up for them by visiting the Blessed Sacrament every day and bringing along some friends if they'd come. Besides The Imitation *I used to read* The Hidden Treasure, *by St. Leonard of Port Maurice. You could read it too, maybe, if you feel inclined.*

You say you don't know whether or not you'll come back to the Oratory. To tell the truth, I also feel that my health is showing alarming symptoms, and I have a strong feeling that I'm going with rapid strides toward the end of my studies and my life. We can at least pray for each other, for the grace of a happy death. Whichever one of us goes to Heaven first must prepare a place for the other and stretch out a helping hand to lead him home.

May God keep us in His Grace and help us to become saints, for we may not have long to live. All your friends are longing for your return to the Oratory and send their loving remembrances to you. For myself,

I remain,

———————

[1] Author of *The Imitation of Christ*

Your most affectionate friend,
Dominic Savio

A tear slipped down onto the letter, spreading out to warp the paper and wet the ink. Massaglia folded the parchment over his heart, as a violent cough racked his body. With a smile, he wondered what it would be like to watch Dominic Savio meet Francis Xavier.

———————

The news reached the Oratory a few short days later. Massaglia was dead. On May 20, 1856, he had gone to behold his Savior Face to face. Don Bosco read the details from the priest who had been at the deathbed to a stunned Oratory.

"He received the Last Sacraments with the greatest edification and died the death of the just man who leaves this world to go straight to his reward."

The sounds and faces around Dominic receded into a blur. Before his stricken eyes appeared the vivid, poignant memories of his closest friend that he would never forget. He saw Massaglia's frank, smiling face on the first day they had met, when he and Cagliero gave Dominic and Angelo a tour of the Oratory. He recalled his feelings of curiosity and respect at finding the robust frame of his new acquaintance kneeling attentively in prayer; the conversation they'd had after Mass one day that had sealed their friendship and the many deep, free conversations after; the riotous games; the countless Holy Hours; the times one had helped the other study for an exam; the pranks they'd played on each other and the occasions they'd stood up for each other. He remembered to the last detail that morning Massaglia had told him he was entering the seminary, and the joy and confidence they'd shared in their vocations. What had come of that? With a sharp pang, Dominic thought of his longing to become a priest. Would that hope, like Massaglia's, never be fulfilled? Yet God had a plan, greater than his own... He recalled his plea to die before committing mortal sin and the subsequent grace he had received of freedom from temptations against purity. Massaglia had been there, too, in that deeply intimate moment. Lastly, he saw once again the carriage rolling off as Massaglia waved goodbye. It had never crossed his mind that he had been looking on his friend for the last time in this life. Oh, dear, blessed Massaglia! Prepare that place for me in heaven that I wrote you to make...

The boys in the Oratory turned their heads in wonder. It was the first time they had heard Dominic Savio cry.

—————

The days that followed saw an unusual change in Dominic. A strange depression arrested his bright, optimistic spirit, almost as if he had lost the will to live.

"Massaglia has gone to join Gavio in Heaven," he often murmured forlornly. "When will I go to join them in the happiness of Paradise?"

His health plummeted. The face which everyone around him had only known to smile was now frequently streaked with tears. If he had been able to cope with Massaglia's illness because of the thought that he too would die soon, then now, the way he coped with his friend's death was by longing to leave the dryness and sorrow of earth. Almost incessantly he prayed for his friend's soul, for though he believed Massaglia had gone straight to Heaven, it comforted him in his desolation to pray for him.

Ah, God! Where were You in those times when nothing smote but evil, when all around was darkness, and the soul cried out to an echoless void and heard nothing, nothing at all? Where were You when death and suffering ravaged the heart like a wild beast tearing its prey to shreds, and life felt empty, meaningless, and painful? When the soul had been rent through with a dagger yet the body had to keep moving on through existence, an alien in a world of hazy, familiar faces, putting on the guise of life yet feeling utterly dead, blasted, *homesick* – where were You then? Did You still care? Did You even know? Did You blink an eye at wrenching away something so good, so pure, so true?

The tensed frame, thinner than ever, fell down at the altar rail, hands clasped, tears flowing.

And the answer spoke, silent yet clear as day: "I was there with you, Dominic, on the Cross."

Light shone in his soul for a moment. Then, having bastioned him for even darker trial, it vanished, and inexplicably heavy oppression crashed over him. He cried out feebly. There was no answer. *My God, my God, why have You forsaken me?* He was safe from temptations against holy purity, but all kinds of other temptations beat upon him tirelessly and mercilessly. Oh, God! Save him quickly! Give him strength! Spare him, Mamma; help, Massaglia! Denser and denser drew the darkness. He could take it no longer – he only wanted to die and slip away from the agonizing miseries of this world – oh, take him, God, for there was only sadness here – but no.

No.

God *did* have a purpose for him here. He would believe it if all the demons and everything in him screamed otherwise. There *was* a Divine design, present in every last detail of his life, even in Massaglia's death, even in this horrible desolation he was experiencing, down to the clothes he put on in the morning and the pen he picked up at school. He would believe it – he clenched his fists – if his soul felt martyred for it. He felt nothing, not the slightest glimmer of comfort. But he would cling to that faith he had been given at Baptism, as the saints had before him in their hours of agony.

This was when love triumphed, when the sacrifice it demanded was a complete death of self, with no feelings to bolster generosity. Dominic dragged himself up to stare at the Tabernacle and wrenched out the slow, tenacious words: "My God, I believe."

For a Christian, perseverance is the last word.

The Sodality of the Immaculate Conception which Dominic had formed with his friends several months ago had never been officially established. They had held several meetings and had built a strong network of spiritual encouragement for each other, but it was not until now that they finally agreed that the rules they were formulating for themselves were complete.

On an afternoon in early June, therefore, Dominic knocked on Don Bosco's door to show him the rules and ask his approval. Among the practices the boys wanted to undertake were the daily Rosary, frequent Communion, correcting each other's faults, spending their time well, and following the rules of the Oratory. Don Bosco read them carefully and nodded his head.

"They look good, Dominic. I'll only add that these aren't binding in any way, though carrying them out will certainly protect your souls from danger."

"Thank you, Father."

"Before you leave."

"Yes?"

Don Bosco motioned to the spare seat and Dominic obediently sat down. The priest's voice took on a gentle tone.

"You've been very sad lately, Dominic. It's not like you."

A tear glistened in the boy's eye. "I know, Father. It started when Massaglia died."

"So I noticed."

"I don't know how to put an end to it. Everything about this life seems so meaningless and I know it's not, but... I'm in such darkness, Father, worse than any I've ever felt. I don't know what to do."

"What have you been doing?"

"Making acts of faith. But they're so hard to say. I feel as if I don't really mean them."

"They are hard often. But that's when they have the greatest value. Keep on fighting, son. Your love will grow very strong in these days."

Dominic nodded submissively, and Don Bosco's heart went out to him. Coming around the desk, he enfolded the boy in his arms, and Dominic buried his face in his chest as his shoulders shook with silent tears.

"Fear not, son, Massaglia is in heaven praying for you," Don Bosco comforted him.

"I only wish I were there, too."

"Now, Dominic, come here." Don Bosco led him to the window.

Through the thin glass they saw the normal stampede of Oratory boys, hard at their usual games and laughter. "See, there is your mission. Your friends still need your company and joy. The time will come when our good Lord will take you to Himself, but for now, He has work for you to do."

"I could help them better by praying for them in heaven."

"Not if God sees otherwise. The best you can ever do is to do well what you are meant to be doing in the present moment."

Dominic stared at the crowd of boys. There was Angelo, making a mad dash with the ball. There was Bonetti, wildly chasing him. Perhaps, if his meaning in life was simply to continue being a friend to them, continue lugging swearers to the confessional, continue striving after that perfection he had always craved...perhaps, after all, he could turn back to his old cheerfulness in all sincerity. His eyes were on the heavens, but his feet were on the ground and would be there for some time yet. So here he must walk. And here he would. Easy? No, not necessarily, but since when had Christianity been known as the easy religion? It had begun with a Cross. Ah, yes, the Cross – there he would find his joy. In carrying his cross in the footsteps of his Master, for love of his King, Dominic would find his joy.

He looked up at Don Bosco, and like billions of Christians before him, smiled through his tears.

———

It was June 8, 1856. A knot of boys stood in the Oratory chapel before the statue of Our Lady, their heads bowed in prayer. Echoing against the rafters on the ceiling rose their strong young voices:

We, Giuseppe Rocchietti, Luigi Marcellino, Angelo Savio, Giovanni Bonetti, Francesco Vaschetti, Celestine Durando, Giuseppe Momo, Dominic Savio, Giuseppe Bongiovanni, Michael Rua, and Giovanni Cagliero – in order to ensure for ourselves the patronage of the Blessed and Immaculate Virgin in life and death, we dedicate ourselves entirely to her holy service...

If Dominic's voice shook slightly when the name of Giovanni Massaglia was not spoken, no one ever noticed. His face was aglow with its old happiness, as he and his friends initiated themselves into the Sodality he had so zealously founded. That Massaglia was not there for the long-awaited day he did not forget, nor did the other boys, but he did not dwell on it gloomily. Nay, for a Christian must not be sad – not when the gates of Heaven are standing open to him. Did Dominic still crave that blissful dwelling? Yes, it had not abated in him in the least, but it was a joyful longing now, rather than a painful one.

His sunny disposition had come back to him like a suit of well-worn clothes, though now with an even more profound dimension of love. He still suffered the loss of his friend, but far in the chasm of his great soul spread that joy stronger than emotion which surfaced like indefatigable happiness yet lay so much deeper. His was the joy of the saint, which the world can never understand though it seeks so desperately.

...Having received the Holy Sacraments and resolved to be filially and constantly devoted to our Mother, before her altar and before our Spiritual Director, on this 8th day of June, do solemnly promise... the boys smiled at each other with shining faces *...that to the full extent of our strength and ability, we shall imitate Louis Comollo[2], we shall perfectly observe the regulations of the house, and we shall edify our companions by admonishing them charitably, and by encouraging them by word and example to make good use of their time.*

It was a moment of grace. Their friendship sensibly dove fathoms deeper. From now on they would be a battalion, bonded by love and promised service to their gentle Queen, and they would fight for her cause side by side, bracing and encouraging each other, even when their military unit was scattered in missionary zeal throughout the world.

Dominic's vehement spiritual anguish had devastated him physically. With his natural excess of energy, he continued trying to compete with the

---

[2]A saintly friend of Don Bosco who died when they were in seminary together and whose example Don Bosco always held up to his boys.

other boys, but the effort only emphasized his growing weakness. He often stopped short in the middle of a game, unable to breathe. Don Bosco watched him closely with an anxious eye.

Toward the end of June, his health bounded back a little and the priest felt a surge of hope. Perhaps that blessed life would remain for many more years to elevate the people around him. Saints would be formed by his example, sinners won over by his genuine, affable ways...

Then he regressed again, further than ever. Distressed, Don Bosco at last decided it was time to send for a doctor.

Doctor Vallauri was a respectable, middle-aged man, well-esteemed in his circle of practice and considerably prominent throughout the city. When he received Don Bosco's note asking for a medical consultation, he immediately sent word to the doctors around Turin, and accordingly, a distinguished trio arrived at the Oratory gates the next day. The typical organized chaos met their honorable persons – boys yelling, boys howling with laughter, boys tackling each other to the ground, all with the energy of young lions dressed in rags.

"Well," remarked Doctor Vallauri, ringing the doorbell, "we were all boys at one point."

"And better off then, too," his friend Doctor Ricci muttered wryly.

Doctor Trimboli adjusted his spectacles in disdain. "It's better to be educated, my dear Signor, and be doing something useful, than to be rolling around in the mud like a badly trained horse. Doctor Vallauri, it appears the doorbell is broken. I suggest you try knocking."

Doctor Vallauri rapped loudly. Within a few moments, pounding footsteps approached and the door flew open. A bright-faced boy appeared before them, poorly but neatly dressed.

"Hello! Are you looking for Don Bosco?"

"We are."

"I'll let him know. Won't you come in?" He held open the door as they filed in, Doctor Trimboli grimacing with disgust at the shabby furniture. "Have a seat. I'll get Father."

He darted off and soon returned with the tall, cassocked priest.

"Welcome, good Signors!" Don Bosco shook their hands with his iron grip. "Thank you for coming." To the boy he added, "Thank you, son. Go run outside with the others. I'll call you back later."

The lad sped out the front door into the yard, where Doctor Ricci watched him fly straight into an ongoing European football game.

"You have a sick patient here, I understand?" Doctor Vallauri began.

"Yes." Don Bosco suddenly seemed very tired. "Dominic Savio. His health was never strong, even before he came, but in the past several weeks, maybe even months, he's been growing steadily weaker. A very close friend of his died last month, and since then he's declined visibly by the day."

Scribbling hasty notes, Doctor Vallauri looked up. "Ah. A melancholic, brooding type, I take it?"

Don Bosco broke into a smile. "No, no. Not at all."

"How old?"

"Fourteen."

"Symptoms?"

"He's lost a lot of weight, isn't as strong as he used to be, he's grown paler, and often has difficulty breathing. When I asked him about it, he told me he usually has pain in his chest and side which prevents him from getting a full breath of air."

The questions went back and forth from each of the doctors until Doctor Vallauri asked to have Dominic brought in. To the bafflement of the three men, the boy who entered was the self same as the lively, cheery youth who had answered the door.

"These are the doctors here to diagnose your sickness, Dominic," Don Bosco introduced them. "Doctors Vallauri, Ricci, and Trimboli."

"Good afternoon, Signors," Dominic said pleasantly.

Doctor Vallauri bowed gravely. Doctor Ricci smiled and grasped Dominic's hand. Doctor Trimboli nodded stiffly.

The examination took place in Don Bosco's office. They checked Dominic's pulse, felt his breathing, measured his temperature, and so on, all the while bombarding him with questions.

"Do you feel frequent pain?"

"Yes, I'd say so."

"Where?"

Dominic glanced up at the crucifix above him. "In my side and chest," he answered softly.

"What does it feel like?"

"Asphyxiation."

Doctor Vallauri started. "Do you know what that means?"

"Oh, yes! It's what Our Lord died from. Suffocation."

Doctor Ricci mumbled something under his breath.

"And it hurts, you say?"

"Yes. Whenever I try to breathe in. The pain makes it hard to get air, you know."

"When does this happen most often?"

"When I'm out playing the games."

"But you still play them?" Doctor Ricci observed.

"Well, yes...but when the pain gets bad enough I usually *have* to stop."

"Naturally," Doctor Trimboli agreed with a bit of sarcasm. "But that doesn't stop you from playing them at all in the first place?"

"Oh, no!"

"Why is that?"

"Why, they're fun!" Dominic laughed. "Besides, my friends would be worried if I didn't."

"They know you're sick?"

"I think most of them do. I haven't asked, though."

"What do you do when you feel this pain?"

"Offer it up."

Doctor Vallauri paused. "Anything else?"

"Yes. I think of our poor Lord and what He must have felt when He was hanging on the Cross. He wasn't only having difficulty breathing, He had also been tortured and outcast and abandoned by most of His friends. Plus, He had all the sin of the world on His shoulders. It's good to put things in perspective, I find."

Doctor Vallauri stammered, swallowed, and nodded. "Yes. Yes. Very good. Er...when else do you feel this pain?"

"Oh, all kinds of times. Sometimes in class, sometimes at night –."

"Does it keep you from sleeping when that happens?"

"Yes."

"How long?"

"I couldn't say. I don't really have a sense of time at night."

"Fair enough. When else are you in pain?"

"Lots of times when I'm praying."

The pens suspended in mid-air.

"Interesting. How long do you pray? A few minutes, maybe?"

"I...I don't really know. I lose track of time then, too."

Doctor Trimboli shifted his feet and cleared his throat. "You can't tell at all?"

Dominic paused, his chin tilted in thought, then shook his head. "I'm sorry. No, I really can't. I don't even think to pay attention to that."

"I see." Doctor Trimboli rocked up and down on his heels and stared at his shiny, brass-buckled shoes. He wasn't used to this kind of case. Better move on to a different subject. "Do you have other symptoms such as headaches, chills, fever, nausea –?"

"Wait a minute," Doctor Ricci interrupted. "Dominic, when during your prayer do you most often begin to experience this pain?"

"I..." Dominic was at a loss.

"Towards the beginning, somewhere in the middle, at the end?"

"Well...very often at the end. I'll feel it when I'm done praying. Though sometimes it'll come on in the middle. That usually happens when I'm less focused."

"Were you less focused before the pain came, or did the pain distract you?"

"I was less focused to begin with."

"Yes. I see." Doctor Ricci nodded slowly and took a deep breath. "So you're telling me that sometimes you only feel this pain at the very end of your prayer, and other times, when you're less focused than usual, you feel it during your prayer."

"Yes."

"Do you think it reasonable to conclude," Doctor Ricci shot an apprehensive glance at Doctor Trimboli, the very image of skepticism, "that in the first case, your body is actually in pain during your whole time of prayer, but you don't notice it?"

"Huh." Dominic looked thoughtfully at the ceiling. "I've never thought of that, but I guess if God wanted me to pay better attention to Him, He could do that."

Doctor Ricci breathed heavily again. "Right. Perhaps He could. Is...is the pain you feel at the end of your prayer the same as what you normally feel, say, when you're in the middle of a game?"

"Oh, no. It's much more intense."

"All right. I see. Yes. That's all. Doctor Trimboli, pardon me. Your questions?"

Doctor Trimboli opened his mouth. The words stuck fast. He cleared his throat and tried again. Mortified, red-faced, shaken to the core, he looked at his shoes again, and suddenly the shiny brass buttons were nothing but a mockery. A jester, jeering at the emptiness of his life, which was all shine and no quality, a noble profession carried out with an ignoble, selfish, shallow heart. And suddenly he was able to speak, and the question that issued from his soul shocked his ears, which had never before heard the voice of that soul.

"Are you afraid?"

Dominic glowed, and his tone was gentle. "No, not at all."

"But...but...surely you want to live?"

"Wouldn't you agree, Doctor, that Heaven is the far better place to live?"

One could hear a pin drop. The doctors looked at each other. Finally Doctor Vallauri scanned his notes and cleared his throat.

"Dominic, Don Bosco told us you were never very strong even before you came to the Oratory. Is that true?"

"Yes."

"How so?"

And so the questions continued. But the angels of God, writing in their ledgers, recorded that it was a far more respectful attitude that the three doctors showed their patient.

At the end of the assessment, the doctors put their heads together and compared notes, speaking in low murmurs, while Dominic serenely swung his legs from his chair and Don Bosco moved steadily through the beads of his rosary. The minutes ticked by. The doctors were perplexed, arguing in confused whispers, but at last they seemed to agree. It was Doctor Vallauri who spoke.

"We can't determine the exact cause of your illness, Dominic, but we do know that you'll have to be very, very careful if you want to preserve your health. Your condition is extremely uncertain."

"Thank you, Signor," Dominic answered. "I understand."

There was not a trace of fear in his voice, Doctor Trimboli noted aghast. Many a time had he delivered that sentence to hear desperate wailing in response. This time, the mind and life flung upside-down was his own.

"The examination is over," Doctor Vallauri was announcing. "Dominic, you are free to go."

"Thank you for your time, Signors." Dominic shook each of their hands courteously and left.

A blanket of silence hushed the room when he had disappeared.

"A gem of a boy," Doctor Vallauri asserted quietly.

"I know it, Doctor, I know it," a broken-hearted Don Bosco replied. "Is there no cause at all you could find for his decline?"

"Well, Father, there is, though it isn't a specific disease we could name. It's partly that he has a weak constitution to begin with, then a very bright and diligent mind that's taxing on his body, and then...well, Father, the intense, constantly strung efforts of his soul."

Don Bosco passed a hand over his forehead. "The remedy?"

"The only way to lengthen his life is to have him put aside his studies and give him some light work to do instead. Send him home awhile, away from the factory smoke of the city. But the best remedy...I hate to say it, Father, but the remedy is to let him go to Heaven. He's ready."

Don Bosco nodded and forced himself to remain hospitable until they had left. But once the door had closed behind them, he buried his head in his hands and his huge shoulders shook with anguish mingled with amazement.

The intense effort of the boy's soul would send him to heaven — oh, God! Merciful God! Dominic was dying of love.

Nine

Two boyish yells of laughter bounced against the rickety fences of Mondonio and swept over the undulating hills.

"Something you wouldn't exactly think of, isn't it?"

"Nah, I don't believe you."

"Why not?"

"No one keeps their kitchen utensils in their pocket!"

"No?" Widely grinning, Dominic reached into his pocket and pulled out a wooden fork and spoon. "There you go!"

Luigi Abruzzo's jaw hit the road, and the two of them burst again into a helpless case of the giggles.

"Oh, I can't believe it!" Luigi groaned, clutching his aching side. "Do you fellows at the Oratory eat that often?"

"No!" Dominic exploded. He panted for breath, attempting to calm himself, then caught Luigi's twinkling eyes and fell into another storm of laughter. "No! We have three meals a day, just like you."

"Then why would you keep your *utensils* in your pocket?"

"Why! They'd get stolen if we didn't!"

"Stolen!" Luigi howled. "Who would want to steal a pair of kitchen utensils? Some desperate character!"

"No, it's true, though! Someone once stole Angelo's. He put them down for a minute and when he turned around, they were gone. Poor Angelo, you should've seen his face!"

"Ha, Angelo! And here I thought the Oratory was a boring place for good kids!"

Dominic choked. "Boring! Oh, Luigi! You really need to visit. You've got some bad confusions mixed up in your brain about us."

"I guess so. But what if they steal my hair?"

"Your hair!"

A black-cassocked seminarian walking down the road smiled dimly at their roar of laughter. He was absorbed in thought — sad, painful thought about the very near future. Oh, God, help him! Be our Savior!

"Excuse me." He had just reached the two boys, who were pounding each other on the back. "Could you tell me where the Savios live?"

From his doubled-over position, still laughing, Dominic straightened and looked up, then let out a cry of delight.

"Michael Rua! What on earth are you doing here?"

He thrust out an elated hand, and Rua shook it slowly, completely dazed.

"Savio?" A smile of astonished joy spread over the seminarian's face. "Dominic Savio!! What happened to you? I thought I'd find you sick in bed!"

Dominic laughed contagiously. "I don't know what happened — Mamma's cooking, I guess. Luigi, this is my friend Rua from the Oratory. Rua, Luigi."

"Is it true," Luigi demanded frankly, "that you fellows keep your kitchen utensils in your pockets?"

"Is that what you were yelling about? I could hear you from the other side of that giant hill." Grinning, Rua pulled a fork and spoon out of his pocket. "Nice try, Luigi, trying to catch Savio in a lie."

"Now tell me, Rua," Dominic urged, poking Luigi triumphantly in the ribs, "what are you doing here? Spying on me?"

"Pretty much!" Rua admitted smiling. "I had to come out this way anyway, so Don Bosco asked me to stop by and check on you."

"Oh, good old Don Bosco. I miss him a lot. Tell him I'm feeling much better."

"I can't wait to tell him! He'll be absolutely thrilled. Are you completely better?"

"No, I don't think so. But I'm not pining away in bed as you thought I'd be, either."

Rua surveyed Dominic with shining eyes. The boy's cheeks were red and healthy and his frame much stronger than the last time he'd seen him. Thank the good God! All the heaviness that had been hanging over him had swept away and disappeared. Dominic was getting better!

Luigi was staring blankly at his friend. "Say, Dom. You were that sick?"

And once again the hills of Mondonio threw back their heads in laughter.

———————

The Oratory welcomed Dominic back with jubilance in August. As the summer vacation ran from July to October, many of the boys had gone home to their families, but those of his friends still there could hardly tear themselves away from him.

"You were gone so long, Savio!"

"I know, I missed you all terribly. What's been happening here? You at least had each other. I didn't have any of you!"

"Well, now, *you* wouldn't know what it's like to be away from Savio for two months, now would you?"

Laughter rang out among the happy circle of friends. Dominic was a leader among them, and they always felt his absence keenly.

Several days later, however, on September 12, Dominic walked up to Don Bosco and asked permission to go home.

"Already!" Don Bosco was startled. "Are you feeling sick again?"

"No."

"Then why do you want to leave?"

"My mom's very ill."

"How do you know she's ill?"

Dominic shifted his feet. "I just know it."

"Did anyone write to you?"

"No, but I know it."

"Ah, I see." Don Bosco had seen his pupil in ecstasy too many times to make light of his request. "Yes, you may go. Here's some money. You can travel by coach to Castelnuovo, but from there you'll have to walk to Mondonio."

"Thank you, Father."

"God bless you."

The coach arrived in Castelnuovo in little less than an hour. From there Dominic began his two-mile trek through the familiar pastures to his hometown of Mondonio. He had hardly left Castelnuovo when he found his father hurrying up the road to find a doctor, his visage distraught with worry.

"Dominic!" the poor, bewildered man exclaimed. "Just *where* are you going?"

"I'm going to see Mom. I know she's sick."

"Go to your grandmother's at Ranello," his father ordered sharply. "Your mother's too sick to see you."

Brigida Savio was in the middle of an excruciating and complicated childbirth. Dominic knew this and understood his father's distress, but he knew also, with driving conviction, that he could not stop at his grandmother's house. He had been commanded to go home. He made straight for Mondonio.

When he reached the house, a handful of neighbors were standing in an anxious, arguing knot by the door. Signora Abruzzo was rushing out of the house; Signora Carabella was weeping bitterly. When they saw him, they threw up their hands in horror and rushed to surround him, insisting that he leave.

"Dominic Savio! Whatever are you doing here?"

"I need to see Mom."

"Oh no you don't! Go right to your granny's! That's where the rest of your siblings are."

"I'm sorry, Signoras, but I can't. I need to see my mom."

"She's very ill, child! She can't be disturbed!"

"I know she's ill. That's why I came to see her."

Respectfully but firmly, he pushed his way past their wringing hands and walked into the house. His mother was lying in her room alone, racked in pain. On seeing him, she gasped in astonishment.

"Dominic!" she cried weakly. Her fingers clutched the sheets in agony. "What are you doing here?"

Dominic smiled. The popular question for the day, that was for sure.

"I learned you were sick, and I came to see you," he answered with gentle simplicity.

"Oh, child!" Touched as she was, Brigida did not want him to stay. "It's nothing. Wait downstairs – no, go to the neighbor's house. I'll call you a little later."

"I will, but first I want to give you a hug."

He hugged her tenderly and kissed her cheek, then left the room. Brigida stared after him in blank shock. Her pain was gone.

"Signora Carabella –!"

"What happened? I don't know what happened – how is she? Is she actually fine or does she just think it? Signoraaaaa!" Signora Carabella's rapid fire questions trailed off in a wail of confusion and exhaustion as the overwhelmed woman plopped into a chair. "What happened?!!!"

Signora Abruzzo's face was pale and subdued as her neighbor had never seen it. "Look at this."

Signora Carabella looked up to find a pink scapular dangling from Signora Abruzzo's gnarled fingers.

"What's that?"

Signora Abruzzo's voice dropped to a whisper, her eyes wide and earnest with amazement. "Listen. Dominic went into the room and hugged her –."

"The young fool. I told him not to go; it simply wasn't proper –."

"Enough, Rosetta. We all told him that. The fact is he went in. And when he hugged her..." Signora Abruzzo began to tremble. "He put this scapular around her neck. And from then on, she was healed."

Signora Carabella let out a gasp of astonishment. "It was the boy! Oh, heaven have mercy on me! He did it, Maria, it was him!"

"I found the scapular as I was adjusting her pillows. She said she'd never seen it before and Dominic must have put it around her neck."

"And now?"

"Now? Why, now she's safe and sound as can be, free from pain and likely strong enough to wash her quilts in the river! And the baby's sleeping like an angel."

"And Dominic?"

"Heaven knows where he is. Probably in the church or playing with the other kids, for all I know."

"And he's aware of the miracle?"

"Don't ask me. You saw his face when he came out – just as calm and unpretentious as when he went in."

"He doesn't have a speck of pride in him."

"No, he doesn't."

Dominic's characteristic humility remained unruffled when he stood before the gawking village the next day as little Caterina's godfather. To all appearance he was the same simply dressed, brightly smiling lad they had always known. To himself he was only an instrument of Our Lady, colossally grateful to her for healing his mother and sparing his baby sister. Mondonio, however, stared at him with the round, reverent eyes of those who know they look on a saint.

After the Baptism, Dominic kissed his mother, hugged his family goodbye, and left for Turin. At the Oratory, he went straight to Don Bosco's office to let him know he was back.

"How's your mother?" the priest questioned.

"Our Lady cured her," was Dominic's candid reply.

Don Bosco smiled and went back to his papers.

A while later, Carlo Savio visited the Oratory and found Don Bosco walking the grounds.

"Ah, Signor Savio, hello! How are you?"

"Very well, Father! And you?"

They fell to talking and naturally enough the conversation soon turned to Dominic.

"I have a question for you, Father," Carlo began. "When you sent Dominic home and he cured my wife, why didn't you ask our permission to let him go or at least let us know he was coming?"

"Well, Signor," Don Bosco explained. "He came to me out of the blue asking to go home that day, and when I asked him why, he replied that it was because his mother was very ill. 'How do you know she's ill?' I asked him. 'I just know it,' he replied. 'Did anyone write to you?' 'No, but I know it.' And so I gave him permission," Don Bosco concluded, a twinkle in his eye, "because my experience has been that when your son asks for something with insistence, I do well to comply."

Another strange event happened later that month. Noticing a slight regression in Dominic's health, Don Bosco decided to send the boy back home for the rest of the summer vacation, as school did not start until November. Dominic accordingly sent his parents a letter to tell them he was coming and shortly later boarded the coach for Castelnuovo. His chest was feeling tight again, and the coach was oppressively hot and stuffy. Two of the passengers were arguing furiously and cursing each other, sending the all-too-familiar pain coursing through his weak body.

"Make them stop, Mamma," he murmured. When they didn't, he conceded, "All right then, Mamma, talk with me so our words can be pleasing to poor Jesus and make up for their dreadful offense."

So they talked on, Dominic and Mary, the whole way to Castelnuovo. They discussed how to convert the newest scoundrel at the Oratory, traveled to Bethlehem and held the Christ Child in deeply loving arms, marveled at the hazy and glorious purple Alps which their King had lavishly made for them, and turned Dominic's constant pain and growing weariness into a resplendent gift to God.

Finally the coach jolted to a stop at Castelnuovo and Dominic unboarded, exhausted and still struggling for breath. The driver lifted down his luggage and drove off. Dominic glanced around. No Dad in sight.

"Uh, Mamma? Looks like we're walking home."

He did love his heavenly Mother dearly, and he did believe that every detail of his life was planned in his ultimate best interest by a Mastermind and guided by his Lady's sure hands. But sometimes, his ultimate best interest and the Mastermind design went through stages that were — well, inconvenient, to put it mildly. Mary very easily could have let the letter to his parents reach home on time, but then, that was her decision, not his. All he could do in this situation was pick up his luggage — oof, it was heavy — and walk home. It was only two miles, nothing compared to what he was used to, but his chest was already squeezing his lungs to suffocation after only a few steps. Praise God, then, for here was a chance to love back his Savior.

Suddenly, an astonishingly beautiful young woman was at his side. Dominic's heart nearly broke with love. Oh! Lovely Queen! Ravished with devotion, he gazed with profound humility and admiration into her affectionate, laughing eyes. I just wanted an excuse to walk home with you, that's all, her sparkling smile read. Then she took the luggage from his hands to carry it herself.

Gentlemanly as he was, Dominic was not about to let a lady — let alone the Mother of God! — carry his luggage, but she gave him a maternal warning glance which said, "Don't interfere, my dear. I want to do this." And off they went, Dominic Savio and Mary of Nazareth, walking down the dusty road to Mondonio.

When Brigida Savio saw her son trudging through the gate at the end of the yard, she was quite surprised.

"Dominic, my poor darling, we didn't expect you!" She rushed to hug him and take his bag. "Come sit down and have a drink. You must be exhausted!"

"Oh, not too much!" Dominic seized the tiny Caterina from his mother's arms and covered her with kisses.

"Did you walk all the way from Castelnuovo alone?"

"No, Mamma." A soft light entered the boy's eyes. "A beautiful Lady met me where the coach dropped me off and was so kind as to carry my luggage."

"Why, Dominic, you should have invited her to drop in and rest awhile!"

"I wanted to, but I couldn't. As soon as we reached Mondonio, she disappeared."

———

"Hey! New at the Oratory?"

"Yes."

"Dominic Savio. I can show you around."

"Nice to meet you! Giusto Ollagnier. And thanks, there are so many people here. I was feeling a tad overwhelmed."

"No kidding. Don Bosco told me there are 199 boarders this year. The Oratory's growing fast. When I came here two years ago, there were only sixty-five."

"Wow." Ollagnier winced as they walked toward the building.

"What's up? Something hurt?"

"Yeah, I've had the worst headache lately."

"No way! Me too!"

"Really?"

"Yeah, Don Bosco won't let me do penances, but I don't even feel like I need them anymore with these wonderful headaches. It's great!" Dominic laughed.

"That's a good way of thinking about it. Don't you want them to go away, though?"

"Oh, for sure. Do you know of any way to get rid of them?"

"Nothing that works."

"Oh, well. Actually, is there any chance you know of a prayer to Saint Aventinus?"

"Oh, the patron saint of headaches! I sure do know of one. I'll ask my dad to copy it down and send it."

"Thank you!"

A unique and amusing friendship arose between the two. As soon as they received the prayer, they formed a habit of going to the chapel every morning to implore Saint Aventinus to free them from their splitting headaches. Several times Ollagnier would enter the chapel to find Dominic repeating the prayer by himself, as well.

Meanwhile, the schoolyear had started up again, and Dominic was attending classes under Father Matteo Picco in the city. On top of his chest pain and growing headaches, he began to develop a nasty cough and consequently had to miss many schooldays to rest. Yet despite these setbacks, he studied his books with the same motivation and perseverance he had always shown, if not more. To the amazement and delight of Father Picco, he consistently remained among the first in his class.

There came a day, however, when his headaches had become so intense he could hardly speak. All through his sickness he had never once been heard to complain, but now he became so quiet that the others couldn't help but notice that something was wrong with their usually cheerful friend.

"Is he all right?" Bonetti asked Angelo and Joey Reano in a low voice.

"Definitely not."

"He looks depressed."

"That's what I thought," Bonetti agreed, "but it's so not like him."

"Maybe he's been thinking of Massaglia."

"Eh, I don't think it's that," Angelo shook his head. "He was talking to me about Massaglia the other day and definitely still misses him, but not in a depressed kind of way."

"Well, what is it then?" Reano demanded. "He's hardly said a word all day."

"Go ask him, Reano," Bonetti suggested. "Maybe we can help."

Reano accordingly walked up to Dominic and put a hand on his shoulder. "What's up, Savio?"

"Not much!"

"You've been really quiet. Anything wrong?"

Dominic tried to smile, only to grimace sharply when he spoke. "It's just that I have such an awful headache that it feels like knives are driving into my temples. But Jesus bore much more without complaining, so I try to bear it patiently." He looked with frank gratefulness at his friend. "Thanks, Reano, it was nice of you to ask."

Reano bounded up the stairs two at a time. Poor Savio had been confined to the infirmary again. School just wasn't the same without him. He kept thinking about those headaches and wondering what he'd be like in such a situation. Knives driving into his temples! Oof, he'd probably be an ogre!

Opening the door to a room at the top of the stairs, he found Dominic warming himself by a fire.

"Hey, Savio! How are you feeling?"

"Why, Reano! Thanks for coming! I'm in some pain, but don't feel bad." He grinned. "Jesus knows I like having things to offer up to Him.

"We missed you at school. What've you been doing? You must be terribly bored."

"Oh, not at all! I've been very busy!"

"Doing...what?"

"Helping out the other sick fellows."

Reano made a face. "You like that?"

"Like it! Honestly, I wish I liked it less so I could have more to offer up! As it is, I like helping them so much I probably don't get any merit from it."

"You really thrive on miserable conditions, don't you?"

They were in a small room which Mamma Margaret's sister Marianna Occhiena had occupied. Auntie, as the boys called her, was lying sick in bed, and Dominic had come to keep her company. She was quite disagreeable that day, perpetually moaning and groaning about her aches and pains.

"Arghhhh, my back! My poor back! This mattress is awful! Ohhhh, oww, why does it have to be me? Argh, I'm in so much pain, and now my head is starting to hurt, too, and my joints are so stiff, and nobody cares –."

Dominic turned on her severely. "Now, Auntie, don't talk like that. Suffering is a gift from God, and it isn't polite to complain about gifts, especially from Him."

Auntie opened her mouth to return a scathing remark but abruptly checked herself in silent thoughtfulness.

Reano darted a swift glance at his friend, struggling mightily to stuff down his laughter. Leave it to Savio to send griping to the moon.

Dominic sat scrubbing one of Ratazzi's giant shoes with a rag. Here was a fellow who really beat up his footwear. Ratazzi had gone to Confession yesterday morning, he recalled with a triumphant grin.

"Why do you do that?" demanded a boy lying in bed nearby.

They were in the infirmary.

"Well, someone has to do it," Dominic replied practically. "And I've got the time for it."

"Doesn't it make you tired?"

"It hasn't yet."

"You're lucky. Everything makes me tired. Savio, I wish I could be like you and be happy whether I'm healthy or sick as a dog, but I just hate being sick. I wish I could just go outside and play football with everyone else or even study Cicero. Anything but lie here doing nothing."

"Yeah." Dominic held the shoe in front of him and tilted his head to inspect it. "But think about it, our bodies can't last forever. Sooner or later they've got to become weak and die, but then! Then our souls are set free and *fly* to their everlasting home, and we enjoy eternal happiness! Eternal happiness – just think about that!" He turned to the boy with a beaming smile. "Being sick isn't so bad when you think of it that way."

"Yeah, but I don't want to *die*!" The poor fellow looked horrified.

"Why on earth not?"

"Because it's scary, and I'd much rather be with my friends and family than – than who knows where!"

"If you're telling me you'd rather be lying here in bed taking medicine every five hours than beholding the Face of God Himself and making friends with all the angels and saints, then one, you're nuts, and two, you just contradicted what you said earlier."

The boy laughed helplessly. "But you understand what I mean!"

"I do, I do. Things we don't know well scare us. But look, we know Heaven's better than earth. So why be afraid of going to Heaven?"

"Well, Savio, I'm not scared of Heaven, I'm scared of the other option."

"That's a wise fear. I guess it's up to you to make that decision now, isn't it?"

"I guess you're right." The lad sighed. "It's such a big and complicated task though."

"Not really. Just beg Our Lady for help and seize every chance to love God that comes your way. And if you miss a chance, ask Jesus for His mercy. You've got to really *want* to become a saint though – that's when you see how pitiful and useless your efforts are and learn to run continually to Jesus and Mary for help. Then *they* make you a saint."

The boy was saucer-eyed. "A saint!" he squawked. "I can't do that!"

"How come?" Dominic grinned.

"Why – why, I'm just a normal kid! I can't become a saint! That's for...for, well, saints!"

"But surely the saints were just normal people too before they became saints."

"Yeah, but...so few normal people do become saints."

"That doesn't mean we can't."

"It does mean we probably won't."

Dominic threw back his head in laughter. "Gee, sainthood isn't a probability! Come on, you can so become a saint. Just think. You were designed for that reason, and you were put in the circumstances that would help specifically you become one. I think you should do it. And so does God."

"You're impossible, Savio." The boy shook his fist playfully. "Honestly, I'd try it except...well, it's hard."

Dominic shrugged and looked him in the eye. "The Cross was harder. And the reward is greater."

The other boys in the sickroom had begun to prop up their heads to listen to the conversation. Some were tossing daunted glances at each other, while others snickered at Dominic's swift, unfazed responses.

"Tell us more about Heaven," one prompted him.

"Now, there's the idea!" Dominic cheered. "Remember the reward. Hmm, heaven. Where do I even start?" He set down Ratazzi's shoe and moved to the sink to wash his hands and fill a basin with cool water. "Well, when I think of Heaven, all I really care to ponder on is that I'll be able to see the Face of Jesus and I'll never have to take my eyes off Him or think of anything else." A dreamy glow had entered his face. "I'll never be separated from Him in any way."

"I guess you'd like that," one lad ventured, "but I'm pretty sure I'd be bored doing that forever."

"Not if you love Him," Dominic answered softly.

There was a silence as he carried the basin to the boy's bed and began unwrapping a bandage around his leg.

"What if..." the boy continued shyly, "what if I don't love Him?"

There was no response. Sensitive heart of a saint! — the question had moved him to the quick. His eyes full and sincere, he raised his gaze to the boy's and held it for an intimate, loving moment. Oh! Love Him, my friend! Love my Jesus! And for a moment, it was as if the lad were looking straight through Dominic's eyes at Someone Else...

With a catch in his voice, the boy whispered, "No, I don't have that question. It's a different one I want to know, and...how do I love Him?"

"Hey, Angelo! Know where Savio is?"

"No, haven't seen him."

"All right, I guess we'll have to start the Sodality meeting without him. Hey Vaschetti! Get over here, you're late for the meeting!"

"Says the fellow who keeps a watch in each pocket with a different time on both."

"Yeah, and you never catch me late for anything, do you?"

"You also look ridiculous."

"Thank you. Have you seen Savio?"

"Nope."

"Argh, where is that boy! All right, we're starting."

The meeting ended with breakfast and still no Savio showed up. In the chaos of getting to classes on time, the boys forgot about him until Father Picco, taking role, lowered his spectacles and called sharply for the second time: "Savio?"

Silence.

"He wasn't around for breakfast either, Father."

"No one knows of any explanation? Is he sick?"

The boys looked around at each other, shrugging their shoulders.

"All right, then. We begin class in the Name of the Father and of the Son and of the Holy Spirit..."

Lunch at the Oratory was full of rambunctious noise as the boys tramped back from their classes and apprenticeships in the city and brought the life rushing back through the halls.

"Hey! Anyone seen Savio? I have something to tell him."

"No, where *is* the kid? I've been looking for him, too."

Bonetti stopped in his tracks and eyed Cagliero suspiciously. "Something's up. I can't find him anywhere. I'm going to ask Don Bosco if he's seen him at all today."

"Yeah, do that."

Bonetti jogged over to where Don Bosco was standing and touched his arm. "'Scuse me, Father."

"Hello, Bonetti!"

"Have you seen Dominic Savio at all today? He wasn't around for breakfast or school or lunch, and I've been looking for him everywhere."

"That's strange." Don Bosco knit his brows. "Did you check the study?"

"Yes."

"And the sickroom?"

"Uh-huh."

"The dorm?"

"Yup."

"Hm." Suddenly the light entered Don Bosco's eyes. "I'll look for him, Bonetti. Go on back to class."

"All right, thanks, Father."

Don Bosco made straight for the chapel. If he knew that boy as well as he thought he did...

The chapel was dim and his eyes took a moment to adjust from the bright December sunlight. Not a sound stirred. Genuflecting, he made his way quietly up the aisle toward the sanctuary.

There he stood, motionless as a statue. Not even his lips moved. One foot was placed in front of the other; one hand rested on a bookstand; and his other hand was held over his heart in a fixed pledge of love. His countenance was turned toward the sanctuary in a glow of transfixed adoration, and his eyes gazed on the tabernacle, utterly lost in contemplation.

Swallowing hard, Don Bosco said in a low voice, "Dominic!"

There was no answer.

He paused. Then again, called louder, "Dominic!"

The boy did not move.

Haltingly, the priest reached out and touched Dominic's arm, then gently shook him. As if waking up from a dream, Dominic blinked and turned his head slowly. Upon seeing Don Bosco, a confused expression came over his face, and he looked back at the pews, puzzled at finding them empty.

"Oh!" he stammered. "Is Mass over already?"

Forcing himself to appear composed, Don Bosco showed him his watch. "See, it's two o'clock."

A deep blush spread over Dominic's face. "I'm sorry I broke the rules, Father," he mumbled, entirely bewildered and humbled.

"Go get something to eat," Don Bosco ordered gently. "And if anyone asks you where you've been, say you were doing something for me."

Dominic nodded meekly and left the chapel.

They had talked about it before, Don Bosco recalled, sitting heavily in one of the pews. It wasn't the first time something like this had happened. In fact, they had talked about it several times.

"What happens when you stay behind after Mass like that?" he would ask.

And Dominic would answer, simply and a little ruefully, "I get distracted and lose the thread of my prayers, because I see such beautiful things that hours seem to go by in a moment."

No, it wasn't unusual for Dominic.

Only this time, it had lasted seven hours.

———————

"Hey, Durando!"

"What's up?"

"I have an idea for our Communion Club."

"Tell me!"

"Well, I know Don Bosco suggested we have a day when everyone receives Communion together, and I'm thinking Christmas Eve Mass would be a good time to do that."

"That's a great idea! Everyone as in our whole club?"

Dominic grinned. "Nope. Well, maybe that's what Don Bosco was asking but —."

"But you want as many people as possibly possible, I see."

"Exactly."

"Both boarders and day boys?"

"Yup."

"How are we going to get the word out?"

"We'll tell the club first, of course, and then get them to spread the news by word of mouth."

"Think people will do it?"

"I'm sure." A huddle of boys were bunched together in a corner of the room, and Dominic looked at them curiously. "I wonder what they're looking at. Tommaso had a drawing of the Holy Shroud the other day. I wonder if it's that."

"Why don't you go check? Tell me if it is. I'd like to see it, too."

Dominic walked over to the group and peered over a boy's shoulder. A gasp — a cry of disgust — a hand flung up over his eyes — and before anyone realized what had happened, he had yanked the paper from their hands and was tearing it to shreds.

Shocked dumb, the boys stared at him and he glared back.

"God gave you eyes to see the beautiful things He has made," he said quietly, searingly. "And you waste them on this trash, which Satan provides to ruin your souls. Maybe you've forgotten what you've heard so often: that one sinful glance stains your soul with sin — yet you go feasting your eyes on the garbage!"

"It was just a joke," one boy muttered, red in the face.

"Yeah, that's exactly what the devil would like you to think, isn't it?"

"But..."

"Sin is never a joke." His eyes were blazing.

"We didn't mean any harm."

"Oh, really? You don't think it's harmful to destroy the purity of your soul so you more easily fall into worse and worse sins?"

Beaten into silence, they darted defeated glances at one another.

"Your eyes are like two windows," he finished roundly. "And it's up to you to decide whether you let in an angel or a devil."

Christmas Eve arrived under a powdery blanket of snow. Distant, shimmering lights floated in the dark blue heavens as on that glad night of old; lights flickered from warm, golden windows in the city and through streaked panes of tall streetlamps; and Light Itself descended into the form of bread as Don Bosco lifted high the round Host over the altar of the Oratory chapel.

The boys whose faces lifted to gaze on that humble Light in disguise were countless in number. Shoulder to shoulder, they had packed the pews to overflowing and were crowded along the sides of the church. Boys in rags, in suits, robust, crippled, teenagers, younger lads, boarders, day boys – they had responded in throngs to the Communion Club's request and now knelt during that joyful Midnight Mass to prepare themselves for God. The candles lit their grave, youthful faces with a soft glow, and the exultant carols from the choir rolled over their heads and echoed against the rafters.

God was an extravagant Giver, thought Dominic. This would be the last general Communion he received with the Oratory boys – and see how many had come! It would be hard to leave them. And yet...he stared silently at that raised Host. And yet he was going to God. For him, nothing could be sweeter. He was going... soon, soon...only a little longer to wait...

An army seemed to arise as the whole church stood up to receive the Eucharist. The boys surged toward the altar rail. Don Bosco turned from the altar. As on that morning in May, they noticed strong emotion in his face, but this time it was of moved joy rather than disappointment. Oh, good, extravagant God, there were so many of them...

Thus closed the last full calendar year of Dominic's life, unbeknownst to the rejoicing Oratory.

January of 1857 came and passed, and February came, and still the young saint suffered worse and worse pain. Still the headaches raged, the cough racked, and his body weakened away. Still classes went on, as did his studies, as did his tremendous prayer. Still he tended the sick and devised unthought-of ways to bring boys to the confessional. And still he smiled broadly and laughed contagiously – perhaps now more than ever – for he knew he was very near to beholding the Face of his Jesus forever.

Ten

Angelo lay on his bed, staring at the cracks in the ceiling. The rest of the boys in the dorm were snoring soundly, but for some reason he couldn't sleep. Turning over, he listened to the sound of their even breathing and the whooshing of the mild wind outside the window. All was so quiet.

Then his ear perked. A suppressed sob had risen from one of the beds on his right. Who was crying? Holding in his breath, he listened carefully.

"For You, Jesus," a voice whispered in the dark. "But it's so, so hard."

Angelo sat up straight.

"Dominic!"

The soft crying ceased at once. A dark head two beds over lifted slightly from its pillow.

"Dominic, what's wrong?"

"I...it's too much to tell, Angelo. Just keep me in your prayers."

Angelo pursed his lips. No friend of his was getting away with that statement. Tossing aside his blankets, he slipped out of his bed and tiptoed over to sit on Dominic's.

"Tell me what's up, Dom."

Dominic pulled himself up and Angelo noticed through a ray of moonlight that his face was stained with tears.

"Angelo!" he sobbed heartbrokenly. "Don Bosco said I have to leave the Oratory!"

"What!" Angelo choked. "No! What do you mean? For good?"

"It will be for good. Don't be afraid, Angelo, but I'm going to die soon."

"Dominic —!"

"I know it doesn't seem like it, but it's true. The doctors told Don Bosco to send me home because last time it made me better, but they're wrong. This time, if I leave...I won't come back."

"Please, Dominic, don't talk like that! If the doctors said it, I'm sure they're right!"

The boy only shook his head.

A sudden chill went down Angelo's spine. Dominic had had strange premonitions before, and every time he had been right. Where he got his information from...well, Angelo knew that. He had seen Dominic in prayer. An agonizing heartache cut through him with sharp, physical pain. Dominic Savio — the best friend he'd ever had — the best friend anyone at the Oratory had ever had — no, it simply couldn't happen! God couldn't do that!

"You've got to get better, Dom!" he wept hoarsely, staring at his friend with two wild, terrified eyes. "Ask God to make you better, *please!*"

Dominic reached over and squeezed his wrist. "Don't be afraid, Angelo. I promise it isn't the end. The people who talk about going to Heaven as if it's the worst and scariest thing ever are all wrong." He smiled for a moment then sighed. "I only wish I could die at the Oratory."

"You really think you're going to die?"

"I know it, but I'm not sad, and neither should you be. I'm only crying because I have to leave the Oratory. I guess I shouldn't get so hung up over it, but I can't help it."

"But...what are we going to do without you?"

"You'll still have Our Lord," Dominic answered gently. "Besides, life is so short. We'll be together in Heaven for eternity before you even realize it."

"I know, I know." Angelo breathed shakily, then gave a short laugh. "I'm such a mess, and here I came over to help you out. I'm sorry, Dom. It's just that...well, you know."

Dominic looked at him with a pondering gratefulness. "Thanks, Angelo. You're a good friend." He laughed abruptly. "Remember that time I got socked by the fellas for not stealing the apricots and you went and got Signor Greco and then he gave us apricots?"

Angelo grinned despite his pain. "Think I could forget? I've never seen a blacker and bluer head than yours that day."

"I've always wondered what you told him. 'Begging your pardon, Signor, but we were about to steal your apricots but instead you need to come break up a fight we started'?"

"Oh, no! I just yelled, 'Hurry, Signor! Savio's getting beat into a pancake again!' and he knew exactly what to do. Grabbed a pitchfork and ran."

They laughed quietly, and Angelo found himself comforted. Good old Dominic was trying to lighten his spirits. What a saint his friend was!

"Say, Dom," he recalled. "You know how we walked to your house after the Di Marzio episode, when I was the one beat up?"

"Yes?"

"You were telling me it's Our Lady who helps you whenever you do any good?"

"Oh yeah, I remember that!"

"Well, I wasn't so sure about it then, but now I know you're right."

"She's so good, isn't she?"

"Yeah. I'm just so glad you told me that, or I'd probably be making no effort at holiness at all. It's such an overwhelming thing when you first look at it, but when you know you've got all the help you need, well, it's much easier to tackle."

"It's so true, isn't it? I used to think I could never become a saint, because I was always comparing myself to people like Saint Sebastian. Then Don Bosco said *God* makes us saints when we simply do our best, and that really keeps me from getting discouraged."

"Don't you ever find, though, that it's hard to do your best?"

"Oh, for sure!"

"Then what?"

"I ask for help, and I get it! But it still does take willpower."

"Yeah, because I guess God isn't going to violate our free will."

"Right."

"I wonder how many people would become saints if they just knew God does everything to help them, as long as they let Him."

"Oh, Angelo! You have no idea how many times I've wanted to lap the entire world just yelling that to people! They'd think I was crazy, but they need to know!"

Angelo eyed him thoughtfully. "Hey, Dom, you've said something kinda like that before, and — well, don't answer if you'd rather not — actually, maybe I shouldn't ask."

"Go ahead. If I shouldn't answer, I won't."

"You said...you've always said, actually, that you...didn't you want to become a priest?"

"I did."

"And..."

"I see your question. Well, Angelo, if I were to stay on earth I would still want to become a priest. And it was that desire that brought me to the Oratory, where I have the guidance of Don Bosco and the friendship of all of you. So I don't believe my desire for priesthood was wasted in any way. In fact, it often helped me take my Faith more seriously. But if I could choose between the priesthood and Heaven...well, it's enough to say I'm not disappointed."

"I understand." Angelo bowed his head in an attempt to hide the grief that had rushed back through his heart, but Dominic was not easily fooled.

"What's up?" he asked gently.

"You sound so sure of it," came the muffled response through fought tears.

"Because I am."

"And that's why I'm so afraid it will happen."

"Aw, don't be afraid. It happens to all of us; it's just a matter of when. You should be glad for me, because I get to see Him so soon!"

Angelo raised two sorrow-stricken eyes to his friend's. "Aren't *you* afraid?"

Dominic smiled, ever so tenderly, as though he were looking straight through Angelo at the Object of all his heart's attention. "Afraid of meeting my Jesus? No. No, I am not afraid."

———————

If Dominic knew he was going to die soon and Angelo half-believed it, no one else really suspected it. Even Don Bosco had strong hopes that he would recover once in his native air. Dominic simply didn't fit the description of a dying person. Everyone knew he was somewhat sick, but he was out of bed so often and so thoroughly his normal, cheerful self that they thought he couldn't be too sick after all. Little did they guess how heroically and carefully he shielded their eyes from his suffering.

If anything caused him pain, however, it was much less his physical agony than the thought of leaving the Oratory, never to return. Of course he loved his family deeply, but at home he could not get the same prayers and spiritual aid that he would here. And if ever he needed them, the hour of death would certainly be the time. In vain he begged Don Bosco to let him stay, but the answer was unyielding. He must go home.

"I'd do everything in my power to keep you here and have you cured," Don Bosco told him, full of reluctance, "but the doctors insist it would be imprudent to let you stay. Believe me, Dominic, I would much prefer to have you here as well."

"God's Will is so hard sometimes," the boy relented, struggling against his overwhelming disappointment. "But I guess that's when we can really love Him. All right then, Don Bosco. For His sake."

The day of his departure from the Oratory was set for March 1st. His meagre belongings were packed up, and word was sent to his parents. A drive even greater than anything he had shown before meanwhile came over him, as he knew how little time he had left. He truly was a man putting his house in order, to the last degree. Every moment with his friends he cherished voraciously, any advice he could offer them he gave eagerly, any time before the Blessed Sacrament he spent in utter focus as though it were the last. Any prayer, any chance to help, any passive sacrifice, the last opportunity to altar serve for Don Bosco – it was a kind of holy frenzy, carried out quietly as always yet with incredible unswervingness and tenacity, even more so than before. Time was running short. Let no chance go unseized...

———————

A knock sounded on the door of Don Bosco's office.

"Come in!"

Dominic entered, the brave soldier's smile still on his face. "Mind if I ask you some last questions before I leave tomorrow?"

"Of course, Dominic, come sit down. What's on your mind?"

Dominic sat down in the worn, faded chair that had been a deaf witness to so many of their conversations. "Well first of all, I want to know how I can get any merit if I'm just lying in bed all day long and can't do the things I used to do."

"Simply offer your sickness and your life to God. It's a good question, Dominic, and what it comes down to is that Our Lord is willing you to be ill at this time in your life, and for your part you just have to give Him back your suffering."

"All right. I'll remember that. And then...what about when I die?" His brows knitted anxiously. "Do you think I'll go to Heaven? I'm worried about all the sins I've committed."

Don Bosco met his earnest gaze with a kind expression of reassurance. "I promise you, Dominic, you will go to Heaven. All your sins have been forgiven."

"But what about when I'm tempted?"

"Tell the devil you've already given your soul to Jesus Christ, Who bought it with His precious Blood."

The confidence that had always graced Dominic's countenance returned. "That's true. I belong to God, just as my name says."

Back and forth went the questions and answers for a long, long time, as the clock ticked and the lamp cast shadows on their warmly lit faces. It seemed as if Dominic never wanted to leave that old, well-familiar room and the saint's presence. So many holy words had arisen between them over his two and a half years at the Oratory, yet now, he knew, these were coming to an end. Like a runner at the end of a race, he stored away all the advice he could glean for the final sprint ahead. Time was running short. Let no chance go unseized. Let no chance go unseized...!

———————

March 1st, 1857 at last dawned over Turin, chilly and clear. Dominic awoke with a strange mixture of sinking sadness and soaring anticipation. What it must feel like to be a few days away from eternal happiness, from seeing the Face of God!

He rolled out of bed onto his knees, and several minutes later was tearing the blanket off Angelo's bed and whacking him with it.

"C'mon, Angelo, you lazy-bones! You'll be late for Mass!"

Angelo groaned and force-rolled himself into a heap on the cold floor. "Mass oughta be at two in the afternoon instead of 6:30 in the morning to give a poor fellow his sleep. I'm gonna have a talk with Don Bosco."

The boys at Mass couldn't help but notice the burning zeal Dominic poured into receiving the Sacraments that day. Not that he had ever done so flippantly, but this was a dimension added even to the ardor he had given before. He was preparing himself for Heaven, now more scrupulously than ever.

Breakfast was a rambunctious ordeal, with a huge crowd of boys surrounding him and demanding so much of his attention that he barely had time to eat. He sat in their midst, listening to them, joking, and laughing his head off.

"There's no way he's gonna die," Vaschetti whispered to Cagliero. "I wonder why he thinks so."

Cagliero knew Dominic better than that and merely shrugged. "It's costing him so much to leave us, though."

Vaschetti eyed the lively boy and whistled under his breath. "Well. You wouldn't exactly guess it by looking at him."

It was a custom of the Oratory to pray the Exercises for a Happy Death each month, and the day of Dominic's departure happened to be the one on which to pray them. After the meal, therefore, all the boys gathered before Don Bosco and settled down to begin the prayers.

Dominic looked round at their warm faces with strong affection. How much fun they'd had together! There was Duina, whom he'd taught to read and write, and Durando, who'd founded the Communion Club with him; Ratazzi, who used to be such a troublemaker but was steadily turning around; good old Angelo, his friend ever since their days back in Murialdo; Bonetti the teaser; Cagliero the noble and impulsive; Rua the serious and devout; Vaschetti the lovable temper-loser; Fabbri and Caputto, who'd almost killed each other in a stone duel; Reano, always the first to rush into an adventure; Roda, whom he'd taught to pray the Our Father. God had been so good in letting him come here. O Jesus, bless his friends and companions!

He turned his complete attention to the prayers for a happy death.

When the time came to pray "for the one among us who will be the first to die," the boys near him heard his tranquil voice saying, "for Dominic Savio, who will be the first to die."

Astonished, they looked at him, glanced wonderingly at one another, then turned back to the prayers.

Dominic made it a point to say goodbye to each of his companions and leave them with some last word of encouragement. In the little time he had left before his dad arrived, he went from one to the next, shaking their hands with his warm grip and wishing them well, always with that same, easy smile.

"Goodbye, Dadamo! You've been going to daily Mass, haven't you? Keep it up! Goodbye, Tomatis! Keep drawing your beautiful pictures for the glory of God! Ah, Ratazzi, my old friend! Do me a favor and go to Confession frequently for Lent, won't you? Goodbye!"

"Bye, Savio! Get better and come back as soon as you can!"

If they were surprised by his words, it was because he spoke as if he would never return, not because the words themselves were so unusual for a teenage boy. They knew him well enough not to be surprised by that.

Giuseppe Momo almost laughed when Dominic placed into his hand a small debt he had owed him.

"Gee, Savio, that was such a small amount of money you borrowed. You know you didn't need to worry about paying it back!"

Dominic shrugged, a wry grin on his lips. "Yeah, but I'd rather not have to explain that to Our Lord. Goodbye, Momo!"

A knock rapped on the wood panel of the Oratory door, and moments later a crestfallen lad approached Dominic and told him mournfully, "Your dad is here."

For a split second, the valiant disguise of cheerfulness dropped as hard reality lashed across his face.

He turned two aching eyes to Don Bosco and asked softly, as if his young heart still clung to that dying hope: "So you won't keep me with you, and I must go to Mondonio? It would only have been a short inconvenience..." Then he shook himself, and the old determination swept back upon his brow. "But God's Will be done. If you ever see the Holy Father, be sure to tell him my message about England. Pray for me, Father, that I may have a happy death, and that we may see each other in Heaven."

"Of course, Dominic."

They walked down the hall, his friends surrounding him; they laughed and chatted as if it were another humdrum trek to class. Vaschetti nudged Dominic, Dominic elbowed him back, Angelo stepped on the back of Cagliero's shoe and kicked it off, and Cagliero almost threw him over his back except that Don Bosco was there. Not a tear was shed, but in the hidden closets of their hearts, swords were piercing.

"Think your mom will bake you those cookies again, Savio?" Bonetti debated. "Those were so good, last time you brought them back."

"She probably did, and my siblings probably ate them all," Dominic answered promptly.

"Too bad for you, Bonetti," Durando whacked him. "We all know you were planning on sneaking onto that coach."

"Aww, how'd you figure that out? 'Cause you were planning on coming, too, huh?"

A roar of playful taunts followed. Cagliero, watching Dominic slap Durando's back in laughter, felt an ocean of respect ebb through his soul. He knew the suffering Dominic was undergoing. O Lord! What a saint! Truly only God could fill a human heart with such fortitude!

Carlo Savio was waiting by the door, dressed in his patched blacksmith clothing. The moment he saw him, Dominic rushed to welcome him.

"I've missed you, Dad!"

"Oh, Dominic! How are you feeling?" Carlo surveyed his son apprehensively, looking for signs of illness. "So sick that you have to come home? Here, let me take your bag."

Dominic handed it to him with a grateful smile and a reassuring pat.

A heavy silence had finally settled over the group of boys who had come to see him off. At last, the nearness of the separation had succeeded in quenching their gallant spirits. Savio would come back, they hoped in it strongly, but there was something about this parting that was markedly different. Just what if, in that ill-defined chance...

"Goodbye, my friends." He looked round at their serious faces with a fond smile. "Pray for me, and may we meet again in Heaven, where there are no more partings."

Angelo gasped under his breath.

On the threshold of the door, Dominic turned to Don Bosco. "Father, would you give me a present as a souvenir?"

"What would you like? A book?"

"No, something better."

"Something for the journey, maybe?"

"That's exactly it! Something for the journey to Heaven. You mentioned a plenary indulgence from the Pope for those who are dying; I'd like to take part in that."

Don Bosco struggled against the lump that engulfed his throat. "Of course. I'll add your name to the list of those who will receive it."

"Thank you, Father." Dominic took his hand and kissed it. "Goodbye."

"Goodbye, my dear son."

And with that Dominic stepped from his beloved Oratory, never to step back into it. The boys called after him and waved as he boarded the coach; they watched as the door shut behind him; the horses started forward with an agonizing jolt.

"Goodbye, Savio! Come back soon! We'll miss you! Bye!"

"Goodbye, everyone! Goodbye, Don Bosco!"

The wheels turned quicker and quicker; he craned his head through the window; smaller and smaller faded the Oratory — and then it was gone.

And only then did he let the tears flooding through his heart spill forth from his brave young eyes.

Eleven

Nine days.

Nine short days to prepare himself to enter eternity. Nine eternities before his gaze could at last rest on that Beautiful Face without ever having to turn away. What a sweet yet tantalizing novena! So near...so near...yet all the more distant because of its aggravating nearness. How intensely his heart had craved the day, for so very long! And now he could almost reach out and touch it.

But was he ready? Dominic stopped in the middle of the road, his hands in his pockets, and stared contemplatively at the fading purple Alps. How could anyone ever be ready for that day? He would be meeting God — the God Who held him in existence, Who had forged those mountains with His Fingers, Who wielded absolute power over the cosmos. He would be meeting that Being Face to face. He, Dominic, an Italian teenager from this tiny, rural town of Mondonio; he, who had nothing to his name but what that God had given him. No, he wasn't ready. Nor would he be ready in nine days when his time was up.

So he would do what the saints had done.

Making the Sign of the Cross, he thrust his soul into the open Hands of his Savior and abandoned himself completely to perfect Mercy. "I am nothing, Lord, but You are All. Take me, Lord, all of me; fill me with Yourself, with Your Mercy. I cannot get there alone."

Oh, joy! No human joy exists like the joy of a saint on the threshold of his homeland! It swept through his soul like a tsunami, strong and deep and overwhelming. Oh, Jesus! You are so close...*so close!*

The next two days passed on dragging feet. Brigida Savio noted with satisfaction that her son was improving. He'd be back at the Oratory in no time, she predicted confidently to her husband. Dominic overheard her.

"Are you talking about me, Mamma?" he yelled from the next room.

"Yes, my fine young eavesdropper! Who else in this house goes to the Oratory?"

Dominic appeared in the doorway grinning. "That's a good point, Mamma. But I'm not going back."

"Why not?" Brigida wiped down a wet dish with a concerned dent between her brows. "You don't like it there anymore?"

"No, it's not that."

"Are the boys bullying you?" A tiger mother expression darkened her face.

Laughing, Dominic took the dish and towel to finish cleaning for her and pretended to pout. "Aw, Mamma, you think I can't fend for myself? Have some more confidence in your son."

"Well, why do you want to leave the Oratory then?"

"I don't want to, but...I'm sick."

"Sick! Listen to you! Eat five more bowls of my good herbal soup, and you'll be off to the Oratory in no time. Don't give me that 'sick' nonsense!"

"But —."

"Ha! No disagreeing with your mother, young sir! Why, you were here sick just a few months ago! And then you got better after eating my soup, didn't you?"

"Ehhh...I did."

"There! Now go off and play with Guglielmo before he drowns

himself in that creek."

Dominic paused. "Mamma, I feel like you should know..."

"What?"

The boy leaned on the counter, torn by pity. How could he say it to her? Yet wouldn't it be worse if she weren't expecting it? His mouth wasn't even working.

Suddenly, Brigida's voice became gentle. "What's on your mind, my boy?"

"Well, Mamma, don't be afraid, but..." His voice cut short.

"But what?" she demanded anxiously.

He looked down at his shoes for a moment, then lifted his eyes to meet hers. Oh! No! He couldn't do it! Not to his mother!

"Never mind," he said with forced lightness. "You're right, Guglielmo's about to drown himself. I'll go keep an eye on him."

He dashed out of the house, and the door swung shut behind him. Brigida stared at it sharply and stood motionless as a rock.

The next day Dominic took a turn for the worse. His cough became more painful and frequent, and his appetite vanished. He acted as sunny-hearted as ever, but his mother, watching him like a hawk, couldn't be fooled. She sent for the doctor, who immediately confined the boy to bed.

"He's not really that bad, is he?" the distracted mother fretted.

"I believe he's much worse than he seems," Doctor Cafassi answered slowly in a low voice.

"How much worse? What is he sick with?"

"I don't know. There's some inflammation, though, so I'm going to perform a bloodletting."

"Oh, my poor child!" Brigida turned white, sick at the thought. "Oh, be gentle with him!"

"Of course, Signora, of course."

The doctor walked into the sickroom grim-faced. He didn't like this operation any more than anyone else, especially when the patient was so young. Most of the time they cried and shrieked and even ran away at that age. Well, he couldn't help it. He sighed and put his bag on a chair. It was a rough world.

"So, Dominic, I hate to say it, but I'm going to have to let your blood." He held his breath, but the lad had kept his unruffled expression. "You know what that is, don't you?"

"Sure do! Are you going to do it now?"

"Yes. Just look out the window, maybe, until I'm done. There, you're a brave lad, I know, but sometimes when they see it happening...you know."

"Aw, Doctor," Dominic smiled up at him. "What's a small cut like that compared to the wounds that went all the way through Our Lord's Hands and Feet?"

Doctor Cafassi halted and stared at his youthful patient. "Er, that's a very good way to see it, you're right. Yes, put things in perspective. Now, if you don't mind me..."

The boy was cool as a cucumber – playful, almost. Flabbergasted, the doctor performed the bloodletting, noting that Dominic was watching the whole process undisturbed.

"You're quite the fearless fellow, aren't you?" he observed, bandaging up Dominic's arm.

"Oh, no, I'm terrified of heights."

"Well that's good, I won't make you climb the Alps to get better."

But he did return to let Dominic's blood again. And again. And again. Ten times in four days he took the boy's blood in the hopes of curing him, but if anything, the blood loss only weakened him further. Yet to Doctor Cafassi's astonishment, never once did Dominic complain or even lose his characteristic brightness.

Meanwhile, the neighbors got wind of what was happening and came in droves to visit the lovable Savio boy. They brought him presents and food (which Dominic regifted to his poorer guests) and sat by his bed to give him the town news and their valuable advice. The youngsters of the village trooped in with their fishing lines and tackle to express their mournful wishes that he could come play with them. Each one Dominic welcomed with warm courtesy, but inwardly he was troubled.

"Mamma," he whispered one night, when the house was finally quiet and his siblings had gone to bed. "Does it bother you to have people always coming in and out to see me?"

"Oh, darling!" the good woman waved her hand. "Don't even think about it."

"But I don't want to be an inconvenience. I'm enough of one as it is."

"Please, Dominic, don't be ridiculous. I just want you to get better. Ease your mind about it."

Brigida gazed tenderly at her son and leaned down to brush his hair away from his forehead. She knew she was biased as his mother, but if it weren't for that, she'd call him a little saint. The dear thing – an inconvenience! Why, he did everything he possibly could not to be. He carried out every smallest task for himself that he still could, he took his medicine without a grimace, and was the same joyful presence to the home he had always been, if not more. No, never an inconvenience, not her precious Domenico. He was the very image of patience. Oh, holy God, spare her son!

"Mamma," the boy said softly, "remember the day you were very sick and I came to see you?"

"Yes, dear, of course."

"I put a scapular around your neck and you were cured."

"So I thought." Brigida's eyes began to moisten. Perhaps she wasn't simply biased, after all.

"What I'm asking you is, keep that scapular carefully and give it to your friends who become similarly sick. It will save others as it saved you."

Brigida nodded.

"Lend it out freely and don't ask for anything in return."

"As you wish, darling."

The glad tidings swept through the village on smiling lips.

"Signora Carabella! Did you hear? The Savio boy is getting better!"

"Oh, Signora! Oh, praise God! Did you see him?"

"Yes, he's laughing and red-cheeked as any healthy boy! His mother told me the doctor's very pleased. He's only been in bed three days now, but we're hoping he'll be able to get up soon."

"Oh, thank the good Lord! Signora! Signora Abruzzo! Did you hear the news?"

Brigida sang as she went about the household chores. The children of the town played and romped with a special vigor, led by Dominic's high-spirited siblings. Carlo Savio walked with a firm, quick step and the old twinkle in his eye. Before leaving for the smithy, he poked his head into his son's room, a broad smile on his face.

"Well, my boy? How are you feeling? The doctor thinks you're improving beautifully."

"I think," Dominic replied in a tranquil, serious tone, "that it would be better to ask the heavenly doctor about that."

"What do you mean?"

"Well, Dad, I think it's time for me to go to Confession and Communion."

"Dominic!" The smile snapped. "But why? You're getting better!"

"I'd rather receive the Sacraments now than be too late," he explained gently. "Please, Dad?"

"I...I...it wouldn't be fair to take up the priest's time," his father argued in desperate confusion.

"Better that than be too late. Please?"

At last the priest was sent for, if only to reassure Dominic's mind. But Dominic was under no illusion. He confessed his sins and received Communion with the most scrupulous devotion and the most ardent joy. Once again, he renewed the four promises he had made at his First Holy Communion, promises which he had repeated very often and which he had never broken.

I will go to Confession often and to Communion as frequently as my confessor allows. Oh, God had been so good to him! He had always made a special effort to receive the Sacraments, but once at the Oratory, they had been lavished on him. He had gone from receiving Communion once a month to every day, because of Don Bosco's blessed permission. And he had gone to Confession every week. What an extravagant gift from God the Sacraments were! He didn't think he'd be half as faithful without them.

I wish to sanctify Sundays and holy days in a special way. Yes, he had always been intentional about going to Mass and offering extra sacrifices on the days the Church set apart, especially those dedicated to Mary. Those feasts had very often helped to rekindle his fervor.

My friends will be Jesus and Mary. Oh, truly they were! They were with him in everything he did, no matter how trivial. How sweet life was when lived in their holy Presence! And not only had he always remembered them throughout his day, but how many times had they visibly come to him! Oh, they were so good, the best friends he'd ever have! How wonderful that he would see them forever, so soon!

And last: *Death before sin.* Not once had he committed mortal sin. Purity had been his jealously guarded jewel, and not once had it been stolen. How many times had he encountered temptations with the force of quicksand – yet not once had the help of his Immaculate Mother failed him. And then God in His tremendous mercy had bestowed on him the grace of freedom from temptations against purity. Oh, how *good* God was!

Dominic opened his eyes on his praying father and sighed in content.

"Now I'm at peace. It's true I have a long journey to Heaven, but with our Divine Lord by my side, I have nothing to fear. Oh, Dad! Tell everyone that if they have Him there's nothing to fear, not even death itself!"

He was radiantly happy. Laughter, strong and genuine, constantly issued forth from his room, where his siblings played and neighbors visited just to be around him. Those in contact with him were convinced he was on his way to recovery, so animated was his joy. If he suffered, they never knew it.

The next morning, March 7, Doctor Cafassi came once again to check on him and perform the last bloodletting of the brutal ten. He was delighted when he found a sturdier-looking Dominic sitting up and telling jokes to his squealing sisters.

"Good morning, Dominic! You look absolutely wonderful!"

"Good morning, Doctor! Thanks!"

Humming and whistling, Doctor Cafassi took Dominic's temperature, asked him questions, measured his pulse, and grew increasingly satisfied.

"We've beaten the illness, son!" he finally declared in a tone of triumph. "Now you've just got to take it easy until you're all cured!"

"We've beaten the world, Doctor!" Dominic replied with an irrepressible grin. "Now I've just got to prepare myself to meet my God!"

March 9, 1857. A day of glory for the Church.

How must it feel to open your eyes in the morning knowing that the same day Heaven will be opened to you? That in twelve brief hours, all pain, suffering, disappointment, frustration, and anxiety will be ended for you? That by the close of that day, your eyes will be gazing on the Face of God forever?

No wonder Dominic's happiness was entirely uncontainable.

Twelve hours.

At noon, his health regressed, and at his insistent request, his parents sent for the priest to return. At the sight of the priest, Dominic's soul broke into song, pure and poetic.

"Pardon my sins, O my God, for I love Thee, and wish to love Thee forever! May this Sacrament which Thou permitted me to receive in Thy infinite Mercy, blot out all the sins I have committed, by my hearing, sight, tongue, hands and feet. May my body and soul be sanctified through the merits of Thy Passion. Amen!"

The priest looked down on him, somewhat confused by his vivacity and serenity. He had attended many deaths, and from what he could gather, this lad was quite healthy.

But Dominic's soul was on fire. Stronger and fiercer that

conflagration was leaping, higher and higher toward its God, toward a place where his body could not follow.

The priest began the prayers for the Anointing of the Sick. Dominic spoke each response with such clarity and intention that the priest felt more bewildered than ever. Why, the boy was more alive than anyone he'd ever seen!

However, while he was still here, Dominic declined so rapidly that he gave him the Papal Blessing.

"I confess to Almighty God," Dominic began, "and to you, my brothers and sisters, that I have greatly sinned..."

No, the priest thought, this soul was pure as a lily. He recited some more prayers and Dominic breathed the responses.

"Those prayers earn you a plenary indulgence."

"Oh, thank God!" the boy cried. "Thank God!"

His soul was secure. He turned his eyes to his crucifix, overwhelmed with gratitude and ecstatic anticipation. Seven hours. Oh God! Sweet God! Come quickly!

Stronger and fiercer that conflagration throbbed, higher and higher that bright and pure flame strained, higher, fiercer, stronger, further — oh, Jesus! So close! So close...

The priest left. Life in the Savio house went on, hesitant but persistent. No one guessed that within those four whitewashed, humble walls, a saint was dying.

Twilight drew its dusky hues over the sky, and the faint stars flickered into the soft purple heavens. The Savios ate dinner. The children went to bed.

At evening, the priest returned to see how Dominic was doing.

"I give my soul to You, my God," the boy was whispering. He smiled calmly at the priest. "Hello, Father!"

"Hello, Dominic." To Signor Savio, he said in a low voice, "I'm at a loss as to what to recommend to him. He seems so well and alive, yet he's acting as if..."

"I know, I know," the broken father replied heavily. "I don't know what to think either."

Somewhat embarrassed, the priest recited a few prayers and stood up to leave.

"Before you go, Father," Dominic asked him, "can you suggest some last thing I should think about?"

The priest paused a moment, then answered, "Think of the Sacred Passion of Our Lord."

"All right, I will. Thank you, Father."

"God bless you, son. Send for me if things get worse."

Nay, they can only get better. Closer, closer — each tick of the clock brings this blessed, waiting soul closer to the Heart of his Creator, the Love of his life. Each tick of that clock cuts yet another thread of those bonds that tie him to this world of sorrow and separation. Quickly, O lumbering time! Speed as never before, for an exile awaits his homeland with towering and intense yearning! Take thy wings and fly! Already the last strands are snapping as his soul strains forth with pulsing eagerness and devouring love — swiftly, swiftly, come to his aid! His heart rests on Mount Calvary, weeping with love at the sight of his Crucified Lord — nay, a heart so pure and strong cannot behold that Perfect Love and remain at a distance — O bring him to his resurrection! — he surges forward! but he cannot, not yet...

A handful of neighbors tiptoed into the house, worried by the appearance of the priest. Dominic hardly noticed them.

"Jesus! Mary!" was all he breathed, over and over again. "I love You!"

And then, at last, his hour had come.

He turned to his dad, who was sitting by his bedside, and whispered, "Dad. Time's up."

"I'm here, son. What would you like?"

"Will you get my prayerbook and read the prayers for a good death?"

"Oh, God!" Brigida gasped, bursting into heart-wrenching sobs.

"Don't cry, Mamma!" Dominic pleaded gently. "I'm going to Heaven."

She choked on her tears and fled from the room.

Struggling to hide his grief, Carlo opened his son's worn prayerbook and began the prayers for the dying. Dominic repeated the words after him.

"Merciful Jesus, have mercy on me...deign to receive me into Thy Kingdom where I may forever sing Thy praises...yes," Dominic added thoughtfully. "Yes, that is exactly what I want. To sing the praises of God for all eternity."

He closed his eyes for a moment. Higher, fiercer, stronger, further that powerful fire leapt – closer, closer – oh, Sweet Jesus! at last! *You are here!*

He opened his shining blue eyes, and a smile of strikingly gorgeous serenity spread over his face.

"Oh! What beautiful things I see!" he gasped softly. "Goodbye, dear Dad! Please don't cry!" His hands were clasped tightly over his blessed, noble heart. "Oh! I see Our Lord and Our Lady waiting to receive me with open arms..."

At last! Oh unspeakable, pounding joy, at last! The last cord breaks – time crumbles to pieces – the radiant soul flies forth to be engulfed in the eternity of Beauty and Perfect Love! O Jesus, Prince of Peace, Mighty and Gentle Savior, my Best Friend – here with You at last! Oh, how beautiful Thy Face – and I need never look away – nay, *never!* How beautiful, dear Lord, how beautiful...

And thus the eternal song of Saint Dominic Savio began.

Twelve

"*Very Reverend Sir,*

Mondonio, March 10, 1857

It is with tears and profound sorrow that I write this note to you, most reverend sir, to convey the saddest possible news. My dear little boy Dominic, your pupil, the spotless lily and new Aloysius Gonzaga that he was, returned his soul to God the evening of the 9th of the current month of March.

His illness was as follows. He took to his bed on Wednesday, March 4, and under the care of Dr. Cafassi they performed ten bloodlettings on him. But while we were waiting to learn what the disease was so we could write and let you know, he passed away. He had also developed a deep cough.

I can't think of anything else, very Revered Father, except offering my regards to you and wishing you every success.

Your most obedient servant,

Carlo Savio."

Don Bosco's voice was hoarse and his eyes blurred as he folded the letter and looked up at the stunned, silent Oratory. The boys looked back, numbed by the shock of the blow. Dominic Savio — that laughing whirlwind of life? How... A sob broke the tangible stillness as Ratazzi, the tough old rascal, dropped his head and wept openly. Others followed unashamed, praying through tears for his soul.

In the back of the crowd, a shattered, hurting Angelo buried his face in his hands and breathed heavily. Dominic had been right. He would never return. Oh, God, *why*? His heart ached so intensely he could hardly think. Why?! His friend from childhood and the best friend he'd ever had, the example that had set him on fire unfailingly — what would he do without him? Oh, if only he could have him back!

Memories happy and poignant swept through his mind, from the sweeping hills of Murialdo and Mondonio to the instances of his friend's visions. Again he saw those blue eyes sparkling with life and laughter, but this time they were only in his mind. Oh, Dom! It was too much for tears. He felt as if he were suffocating.

For some reason that night he'd heard Dominic crying kept coming back to him.

"You said..." he heard himself stumbling, *"you've always said, actually, that you...didn't you want to become a priest?"*

"I did."

"And..."

"I see your question. Well, Angelo, if I were to stay on earth I would still want to become a priest... But if I could choose between the priesthood and Heaven... well, it's enough to say that I'm not disappointed."

Over and over it played in his memory, and he had no idea why. Poor Dominic had never become a priest. What a good one he would have made! Angelo would have liked to go to Confession to him every day if only to get his ever practical advice. As for himself, he'd never cared about becoming a priest, but seeing the way Dominic wanted it had always been so beautiful. It almost made him open to the possibility... Dominic had always had that effect on people. He did or wanted something, and inevitably everyone else did or wanted it.

But Angelo knew distinctly that this was different. Either he was overwhelmed with suffering and it was messing with him, or — terrifying, startling thought — God was truly calling him. Whatever it was, he didn't like it. "You'd do better to choose someone else, Lord," he squirmed. "I'm such a dud of a fellow. Don't pick me, *please.*"

"If you wish to be perfect, go, sell what you have and give to the poor. Then come, follow Me."

Dominic had always desired to be perfect. And Angelo had always wanted to be like Dominic. But this had been Dominic's vocation, not his — or, rather, it hadn't really been Dominic's vocation, but it certainly wasn't Angelo's! But the voice in his heart persisted.

"If *you* wish to be perfect..."

Oh, if only Dominic had been there to help him sort out this disaster! He missed his friend acutely. Oh, Dominic, why did you leave? I still need you.

But then, he realized Dominic was still there. He was no less a friend in Heaven, only a more powerful one. And he had finally received what his heart had so long yearned. Who was Angelo to lament the happiness of his best friend? Yes, his best friend, for he had been hugely graced with the intimate friendship of a saint.

And good old Angelo, the brave and steadfast friend since the beginning, threw up his head and leaping to his feet, shouted triumphantly, "*Saint* Dominic Savio, pray for us!"

The cry echoed through the room above the sobs of the mourners and swept up to the heavens, to the ears of the Church's newest saint and the beloved Oratory boy.

"Saint Dominic Savio, pray for us," Cagliero whispered through his tears.

A knot of Sodality boys praying for his soul halted and glanced hesitatingly at one another.

"Saint Dominic Savio, pray for us!" one of them suddenly cried out.

And all at once, the Oratory shook with the cry, firm and elated beyond grief. Someone held up a rosary that had belonged to him and kissed it, and a wild stampede rushed through the building to find things he had owned to keep as relics. Tears ceased, replaced by crazed joy and excitement.

They had lost a companion, perhaps, but in place they had received a saint.

Epilogue

Two seminarians stood against the wall. In a room of shouting, leaping boys and amazed expressions, they and Don Bosco alone remained unsurprised. Oh, it was a wondrous thing, for sure, but what else would you expect from Savio, especially when you'd been friends with him growing up?

One smiled broadly and shook his head.

"Leave it to Savio," he muttered to the other. "It isn't the first time, and it won't be the last."

The other seminarian merely bowed his head in prayer as a deep wave of joy rolled into his soul.

"Three cheers for Savio!" the boys were yelling. "We knew he was a saint!"

A dozen hands reached to help the bewildered and ecstatic Davico from bed, but Don Bosco stopped them.

"No!" he ordered, over the chaos of jubilance and astonishment. "If he wants to be cured, he'll have to get up himself."

The commotion trickled to a hush. It might be too much for him — there would be a relapse —.

"Nonsense," Don Bosco said firmly. "Come on now, Davico, get up!

Dominic Savio doesn't do things by halves!"

Davico looked up, a determined glint in his eye, as the doctor groaned audibly. Then with a bound, he was up and standing on two sturdy feet and laughing in delight, as the boys sent up a howl of applause bursting with pride for their Savio, even louder than before.

"Come on, Davico, let's play ball!" they roared with glee. "You're cured, old boy, look at you! Let's go! Savio's a saint!"

The two seminarians watched them storm outside, thinking of the days they'd run around in a crowd like that with Dominic. How blessed they had been to know him!

"I always thought of the saints as lofty and not very human," Bonetti confided to a smiling Angelo. "But now I think differently. He was so down to earth and more human than any of us."

"Yet so holy!" Angelo reminisced. "Did you know even Don Bosco asked for his advice and followed it?"

"Don Bosco! Why, no one ever told me that! Now there's another saint."

"Yeah, think of that, Bonetti. We've known two saints during our lifetime. Some people brag if they've glimpsed one from afar."

"Yet...the way they became saints..."

"What about it?"

"They're both so normal. You'd think more people would be saints, if they just lived their lives to the full like Savio and Don Bosco."

"'Extraordinary virtue in ordinary life,'" Angelo quoted. "Isn't that what Don Bosco says? Or was it Saint Francis de Sales?"

"Probably both. But whoever said it is spot on. And that's exactly what Savio did."

That night, Bonetti sat down at his desk, lit a candle, and opened his journal. A million thoughts were spinning through his brain, and he needed to sort them out.

Extraordinary virtue in ordinary life. If that was all it took, maybe he could handle it. He probably wouldn't be levitating off the ground or rushing around hospitals to nurse the sick without stopping to sleep, but then, Savio hadn't either. And Savio had done it.

It was remarkable when he stopped to think about it. He had known a saint. He had lived with one for two and a half years. A saint his own age. They had played sports together, sat in class together, walked to church together, prayed together, ate their meals together. All the normal human things that Bonetti did, Dominic had done, too. Dominic had lived at the same time, in the same country, in the same building as he did. He'd eaten the same porridge, known the same friends, listened to the same teachers, walked the same grounds.

It was so real to Bonetti, all of a sudden, that mysterious thing people called sainthood. Extraordinary virtue in ordinary life. It was so tangible and attainable, and all at once Bonetti thought that even to those who would never know Dominic as he had, sainthood would still appear in its true simplicity through his humble example. Even if he hadn't shared so many circumstances with Dominic, one thing would remain: that it was God Who formed saints and not self, for God used human efforts and normal human life to create breathtaking Divine masterpieces.

Bonetti sat back, his hand cramped from writing. He looked up at the crucifix that hung over his desk. Yes, the Risen Jesus had wrought victory in Dominic Savio, and He would do it in many, many others, as many as desired and pursued it.

The trembling youth picked up his pen again and bent over the paper. His hand scratched five triumphant words in Latin.

Sic ille, cur non ego?

If he became a saint, why not I?

Author's Note

See the picture: a boy kneeling low before the altar, lost in prayer, while the rest of his friends noisily congregate outside the church. After a long time, he slowly gets up, and slowly walks away, turning every now and then to bid a loving parting to his Eucharistic Lord. Then he steps outside and his friends immediately surround him in delight. He laughs with them and teases them, but ever in his heart, his gaze is still upon that Divine Face hidden in the tabernacle. From thence his life flows.

And what a life!

This is the picture I've tried to paint of Dominic Savio — a boy whose heart always dwelt in God's, a boy who loved Jesus Christ first and then his friends, a boy simultaneously normal and extraordinary. If I've even scratched the surface of who he was, it was only because of the goodness and inspiration of the Holy Spirit.

My aim in writing this book was to bring out Dominic's lovable personality, to portray him as the spirited, high-idealed, and uncompromisingly devoted yet perfectly normal young person he was. There was an unbreakable strength in his character which I believe people often overlook because of his physical weakness. Yet take a moment and recall the classic image of a slight youngster stepping with raised crucifix between two murderous stone duelists. It reminds one of St. Stephen, the first martyr, stoned to death. There's nothing weak about it.

I found that to bring the person of Dominic Savio to life, I had to write this book as a story rather than a strict biography. That being said, every story in here is based on facts known about his life, but some stories are more exact than others. For example, Fr. Peter Lappin, a Salesian of Don Bosco, writes in his book *Dominic Savio: Teenage Saint* that "Dominic's determination showed itself frequently during his early life...with the boys of the village who beat him for not doing something against his conscience." Fr. Lappin also records that Dominic always refused "to go along with [the village boys] on their usual escapes – throwing stones, breaking into orchards, or making fun of old people... He had continued to refuse even when the bigger boys threatened to punch his nose for not going." From these lines I wrote the story of Signor Greco's apricot orchard. On the whole, each of these stories are based on something which Dominic was known to do; I've done everything I could to keep his essential actions and habits intact while providing details such as settings and characters to give the book a sense of reality.

Another example of this is in his visions. The ecstasies in which Don Bosco found him and the vision of England happened as written, but those which occurred amidst his friends are less exact. It is true, however, that he fell into ecstasy at any given time of day – in class, speaking with his friends, and most especially after receiving Communion. It's also true that these caused him embarrassment, and he often walked away when they came so as not to appear "ridiculous" in front of his friends.

The conversions in this book are likewise based on commonly used strategies of that young mastermind Savio, but some of the characters involved I've had to create. Don Bosco claimed that these tricks of Dominic's were more effective than many a homily; Professor Bonzanino, of a similar mind, seated unruly students near Dominic and always noted significant changes in them. Any conversions which Don Bosco records I've included here. Many boys did transform their lives because of his words and example, above all because of his persistent drive to get them to the Sacraments. Ratazzi, for instance, was a hardcore troublemaker (and Dominic did once get into a fight with him) but the next time he punched Dominic, the saint's self-control won him over and marked the beginning of his conversion back to the Faith.

For those like myself who like to know the true parts of truth-based stories, I've included below a very brief summary of which major events were historically accurate. It's my hope, however, that you will not disregard parts of this book because they did not historically occur word for word. Any events that I recount here which weren't "historical" were actually habits of Dominic, which occurred so frequently that Don Bosco spoke of them in general terms rather than relating specific examples. For that reason, it just wouldn't be fair to Dominic to overlook the stories more shrouded in my artistic liberty, because similar incidents happened all the time, and thus tell more about him than less.

The following characters were historical people: St. Dominic Savio and St. Don Bosco (hopefully you knew that already), Mamma Margaret, her sister "Auntie" Marianna Occhiena, the Sodality boys (Giuseppe Rochietti, Luigi Marcellino, **Giovanni Bonetti**, **Francesco Vaschetti**, **Celestine Durando**, Giuseppe Momo, **Giuseppe Bongiovanni**, **Michael Rua**, and **Giovanni Cagliero**). The names in bold are of those who went on to become priests. The other historical Oratory boys were Antonio Duina, whose conversion happened mostly as written; Davico; Ratazzi; Giusto Ollagnier, who did pray to St. Aventinus with Dominic; Tomatis, an amateur artist who later drew a picture of his departed friend; Giuseppe Reano; Giovanni Roda-Ambre, whose conversion happened mostly as written; and Camillus Gavio. The names and ages of all Dominic's family members are true to fact. Doctors Vallauri and Cafassi were real-life men who played the said roles in Dominic's life, as were any priests and teachers mentioned by name. Angelo Savio was a close but unrelated family friend of Dominic in Murialdo, then Mondonio, and finally at the Oratory. While his name is not actually recorded in the list of boys who formed the Sodality (I added him), Dominic did speak to him frequently about his desire to become a priest and Angelo did end up becoming one himself. Giovanni Massaglia, another Oratory boy, was Dominic's closest friend, who died while in seminary in the way recounted here. The names of the village people are not factual, though such people did exist and draw much from Dominic's life. They were among the first to recognize his sanctity and jealously guarded his body when he died. Many other characters in this book were real people who had the described interaction with Dominic, only their real names are not known. Examples are the stone duelists and Di Marzio. Other characters are entirely fictional, but their roles in Dominic's life are examples of roles which real people were known to play.

Any place mentioned by name did exist and did contain the ascribed events. Any exact date was the actual date of the events it contains (for instance, the Sodality was founded on June 8, 1856, and Dominic died on March 9, 1857, etc.).

Other notes. Dominic did kneel in the snow (or any kind of weather, for that matter) before the church to wait until it was unlocked as a young boy. The episode in which his guardian angel carried him home did occur. From a very young age, he wanted to become a priest, which caused him to insist on continuing his education, even though it was financially difficult for his family and the roads were long and dangerous. For that reason, the neighbors did put up a farmer to convince him from continuing the trip to school, and the subsequent conversation occurred as written. The episode with Di Marzio and Dominic's temporary disgrace did happen. Any spiritual progress in Dominic at the Oratory played out as written, beginning with a homily by Don Bosco which marked a significant ascent in Dominic's holiness, as it inspired him to become a saint. The conversations between Dominic and Don Bosco almost entirely happened as written. Dominic did feel physical pain at hearing others swear, which Don Bosco wrote contributed to his eventual death. He also received headaches through his violent effort to keep his eyes down while walking through the streets. Most of the conversation with Gavio when they first met, Dominic's care for his dying friend, and Gavio's subsequent death did occur. The mysterious finding of the plague victims and the cure of his mother happened as written. As to the woman dying in the closet, it is not known whether or not Our Lady appeared to him prior, but Fr. Lappin records that Dominic responded to the owner's confusion as if he knew exactly what house to look for. Considering the frequency of his visions and the conviction of his answer to the houseowner, it's not unlikely that a grace revealed an image of the house to him. We don't know exactly when and how Dominic's final and gradual decline in health began, but it was several months before his death. Before that, he had often been sick as well. Michael Rua testified that Dominic eventually won complete protection against temptations against purity, but how and when he received that grace I don't know. I connected the grace to another real event in which Dominic did go into a vision and faint as a result of one of Don Bosco's evening talks on purity. The death of Massaglia occurred as written, his correspondence with Dominic is almost word for word (as is any letter, manuscript, or document included here), and Dominic's subsequent heavy sadness was something the Oratory had never seen in him before. The medical consultation with Dr. Vallauri is not word for word; however, Don Bosco writes that the doctor was very impressed with Dominic's answers and bright disposition, and the doctor's parting words with Don Bosco are as written. While no one knows for certain the cause of Dominc's death, Dr. Vallauri attributed it to the constant efforts of his soul. This "diagnosis" and Dominic's parting words cause me to believe that he died of love. Fr. Gaitley writes that St. Therese, as well, suffered of tuberculosis but died of love. Both were "little souls" with great love (not to mention saints); therefore, I see no reason why this wouldn't be the case for Dominic. The fact that he was so healthy up to his last hour confirms my belief in this. It is also true that he counted down the days and hours to his death. I don't know for sure if he had tightness and pain around his chest, but critics have suggested pleurisy or pneumonia as Dominic's illness, based on his symptoms, and these would then have been symptoms. The other symptoms here described are as chronicled by Don Bosco.

During Dominic's journey from Castelnuovo to Mondonio, Our Lady did appear to him and carry his luggage, then disappearing when they reached the village. The scene in which Dominic tore up the pornographic image did occur; then the boys argued with him and he easily shut them down; and his final quote of the scene is one he would often say (about the eyes being windows). Dominic did care for the sick during his illness and loved doing it;

he talked with them about Heaven and performed humble tasks such as cleaning shoes to keep himself occupied. Almost all the details about Dominic's departure from the Oratory, the final nine days of his sickness, and his death occurred as written. The letter here written to inform the Oratory of his death was read by Don Bosco to the boys, most of whom responded by praying *to* rather than *for* him and by searching for his belongings as relics. Later, the cure of Davico (and many others) was obtained. Don Bosco often preached to his Oratory on the life of Dominic Savio, and as a seminarian, Giovanni Bonetti wrote the book's final Latin words about his late friend in his diary.

May Saint Dominic Savio pray for you, and may his blessed example encourage you to sainthood! If God made him a saint, He can make you one, too.

Made in United States
Cleveland, OH
16 February 2025

14405572R00125